Lisbon

Portugal

EVERYMAN
CITY GUIDE

EVERYMAN CITY GUIDES
Copyright © 1998 David
Campbell Publishers, London

ISBN 1-85715-863-6

First published April 1998

Originally published in
France by Nouveaux Loisirs,
a subsidiary of Gallimard,
Paris 1998, and in Italy by
Touring Editore, Srl.,
Milano 1998.
Copyright © 1998
Nouveaux Loisirs,
Touring Editore, Srl.

SERIES EDITORS
EDITORIAL MANAGER:
Seymourina Cruse
LISBON EDITION:
Caroline Cuny, Mélani
Le Bris, Seymourina Cruse
GRAPHICS
Élizabeth Cohat, Yann Le Duc
LAYOUT:
Silvia Pecora
AIRPORT MAPS:
Kristoff Chemineau
MINI-MAPS:
Studio Wise
AROUND LISBON MAPS:
Édigraphie
STREET MAPS:
Touring Club Italiano
PRODUCTION
Catherine Bourrabier

Translated by Michael Mayor
and Ruth Blackmore
Edited and typeset by Book
Creation Services, London

Printed in Italy by
Editoriale Libraria

Authors
LISBON

Things you need to know:
Madeleine Gonçalves (1)
Her Portuguese origins and knowledge of
the country make M. Gonçalves the
perfect source of all practical travel
information.

Where to stay:
Isabel Azevedo (2)
A graduate of the School of Hotel
Management in Lausanne, I. Azevedo is
an expert on the wide range of
accommodation available in Lisbon.

Where to eat:
David Lopes Ramos
D. Lopes Ramos is the editorial writer
for the society page of *Público*, and also
co-author of a guide to Portuguese
restaurants, published in 1998. He did
not wish to be photographed.

After dark: Rui Catalão (3)
Following his studies at the Universidade
Autónoma de Lisboa, R. Catalão has,
since 1995, contributed articles to the
Público music supplement *Sons*.

What to see & Further afield:
Vítor Wladimiro Ferreira (4)
A writer and lecturer, V. W. Ferreira has
long been responsible for introducing
Portuguese culture to a wider audience.

Vítor Serrão (5)
A professor of art history and a
champion of Portuguese culture, V. Serrão
has been on the board of the National
Council for Culture since 1996.

Jean-François Chougnet (6)
J.-F. Chougnet became interested in
Portugal and the Portuguese at a very
early age. He first went to Lisbon at 17,
and has since been a frequent visitor.

Where to shop:
Isabel Coutinho (7)
A journalist on the daily *Público* since
1992, I. Coutinho writes on changing
fashions, movies, and current literature.

*Note from the publisher:
To keep the price of this guide as low as
possible we decided on a common edition for
the UK and US, which has meant
American spelling.*

Contents

Symbols

- ☎ telephone number
- ➡ fax number
- ● price or price range
- 🕐 opening times
- ▤ credit cards accepted
- 🚫 no credit cards
- 🆅 toll-free number
- @ e-mail
- ★ hot tips and advice

Access

- **M** nearest subway(s)
- 🚌 bus (or tram)
- **P** private parking lot
- 🅥 valet parking
- ♿ no facilities for the disabled
- 🚆 train
- 🚗 car
- ⛴ boat

Hotels

- ☎ telephone in room
- 📠 fax in room on request
- 🍸 mini-bar in room
- 📺 television in room
- ❄ air conditioned in room
- 🕐 24-hour service
- 🛎 porter
- 👶 child minding, babysitting
- 🚪 meeting room(s)
- 🐾 no pets
- ☕ breakfast
- ☕ afternoon tea
- 🍴 own restaurant
- 🎵 live music
- ● nightclub
- 🌳 garden, patio or terrace
- 🏋 gym, health club
- 🏊 swimming pool, sauna

Restaurants

- 🥗 vegetarian dishes
- 👁 outstanding views
- 👔 smart dress required
- 🚬 smoking section(s)
- 🍸 bar area

Sightseeing

- 🎁 gift stores
- 🚩 guided tours
- ☕ cafeteria

Shops

- ↔ branches, succursales

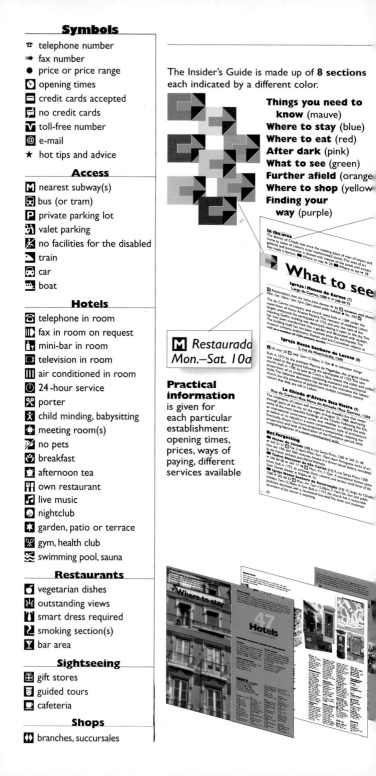

The Insider's Guide is made up of **8 sections** each indicated by a different color.

Things you need to know (mauve)
Where to stay (blue)
Where to eat (red)
After dark (pink)
What to see (green)
Further afield (orange)
Where to shop (yellow)
Finding your way (purple)

Practical information is given for each particular establishment: opening times, prices, ways of paying, different services available

How to use this guide

In the area

The district of Chiado was once th ...sbon home to some of Lisbon's most so ...ores is dotted with statu ... ◼ Where to stay ➡ 2(

The section **"In the area"** refers you (➡ 00) to other establishments that are covered in a different section of the guide but found in the same area of the city.

Chiado   **A** B-C 2

P.L.de **21**
amões **8**   **13**
ecrim **12**   oso   **19**   R u a   G arr

The small map shows all the establishments mentioned and others described elsewhere but found "in the area", by the color of the section.

The name of the district is given above the map. A grid reference (**A** B-C 2) enables you to find it in the section on Maps at the end of the book.

museum contains prehistoric, Rom
well as a number of 12th-century

Hot tips, indicated by a star ★, contains advice from the author: the best rooms, recommended dishes, views not to be missed...

Not forgetting

◼ **Museu do Chiado (10)** 6, ...
➡ 343 21 51 ◻ Tue. 2–6pm; Wed...

The section "Not forgetting" lists other useful addresses in the same area.

The opening page to each section contains an index ordered alphabetically (Getting there), by subject or district (After dark) as well as useful addresses and advice.

The section "Things you need to know" covers

information on getting to Lisbon and day-to-day life in the city.

Theme pages focus on a particular topic.

The "Maps" section of this guide contains 6 street plans of Lisbon followed by a detailed index.

Time difference

Lisbon is on GMT. The clocks go forward on the first of April and back on the first Sunday of October.

➤ Getting there

Pets

Pets are not allowed in most hotels and restaurants. There are, however, no particular restrictions on taking them into the country.

Voltage

The electrical current is 220 volts. You will need an adaptor to use British plugs.

Tourist office

In USA: *590 Fifth Avenue, 4th floor, New York, NY 10036* ☎ *(212) 354 4403*
In UK: *22–25a Sackville Street, London W1X 1DE* ☎ *(0171) 494 1441*
The Tourist Office does not make hotel reservations but offers a wide range of information to help you prepare for a trip to Lisbon or Portugal.

35 Things you need to Know

Passports

Portugal became a member of the European Union in 1986 and there are therefore no limits on the length of stay for any EU national holding a valid passport. Visitors with US or Canadian passports can stay in Portugal for up to 60 days without a visa. Visitors from other countries may require a visa and should enquire at the Portuguese consulate or embassy in their home country before leaving.

Medical care

All EU nationals qualify for free medical treatment on production of an E111 form (available from social security and post offices). Visitors from other countries are advised to take out travel insurance. In an emergency ➡ 15.

Basic facts

TAP, TWA and Delta operate regular scheduled flights to Lisbon from New York. There are also direct flights from Boston and Miami. It is possible to get budget flights to Spain or London and pick up cheap flights, or buses there. TAP and British Airways have flights from London

Getting there

Information

Lisbon's international airport, Portela de Sacavém, is just 4 miles northeast of the city.

Switchboard
☎ 841 35 00

Arrivals and departures
☎ 841 37 07

Tourist information
The airport has a small Posto de Turismo (tourist information office) which can give you hotel information, a map of Lisbon, and route maps.
☎ 849 36 89
➡ 848 59 74
🕒 open daily 6am–2am

Lost property

The lost property office in the airport is located in the departure terminal just before the

check-in desks.
☎ 849 61 32
🕒 open 24 hours
There is also a lost and found office in the arrival terminal.
☎ 841 54 17

Police

The PSP (Polícia de Seguranca Pública) has two offices, one in the arrival terminal, the other in the departure terminal
☎ 849 61 32
🕒 open 24 hours

Telephone

The airport has pay phones in several locations (they take a minimum of Esc. 20), as well as card phones. You can buy phone cards from the newspaper stands in the airport.
● Esc. 875 (50 units), Esc. 2100 (120 units)

Currency exchange offices

The Banque Totta & Açores, located in the arrival terminal, can change money and also has Multibanco cash dispensing machines which accept many international credit and debit cards.
☎ 842 14 70
🕒 Mon.–Fri. 7.30am–6am
There are also a number of 24-hour currency-exchange offices next to the bank.

Post office

There is a post office in the Corpo Sul area near the departure terminal.
🕒 open 24 hours
Another post office is in the departure lounge.
🕒 7am–5pm, 5.30–8pm

Airline companies

TAP-Air Portugal
☎ 841 69 90
is the Portuguese national airline. For some local flights it uses its subsidiary airline, LAR.

Getting from the airport to the city center

Aero-bus shuttle service
An express bus (no. 91) stops just outside the international arrival terminal and shuttles between the town and the airport. It terminates in Cais do Sodré stopping off en route at Entrecampos, Saldanha, Avenida da Liberdade, Restauradores, Rossio, and Praça do Comércio. The

(Heathrow) and TAP flies from Manchester to Lisbon.

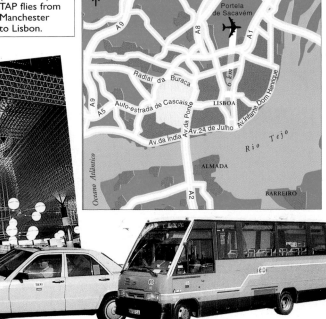

trip takes about 30 minutes. It is a very convenient way to get to the center and the bus has plenty of room for luggage. Buy your ticket on the bus. If there are more than two of you traveling together, a taxi is probably a cheaper option.

● *There are two kinds of ticket: a day travel ticket (Esc. 430) or a three-day travel ticket (Esc. 1000), both of which are also valid for other forms of transportation. Individual tickets are not available.* ◷ *7am–9pm Buses depart every 20 mins.*

Passengers who have traveled with TAP-AIR, the Portuguese airline, are entitled to a complimentary ticket. Claim this by presenting your

ticket at the TAP desk in the arrival terminal.

City buses

The 44, 45 and 83 buses all go to the center, stopping off en route at the main squares. They depart from the main road outside the airport. The trip takes about 30 minutes.
● *Esc. 150*
◷ *6am–midnight Buses depart every 20 mins. They are not the best option if you have lots of luggage as they are often fairly full.*

Taxis

Taxis wait just outside the airport entrance and are available round the clock. They are either black and green or beige. The trip takes around 15-20 minutes if the traffic is good. All taxis have meters. The minimum

fare is Esc. 250 and a charge of Esc. 300 for luggage is added on. The trip costs on average:
● *Esc. 1500*

Hotels

There is no hotel in the airport itself, but there is a good one nearby. A taxi ride of about 5 minutes will get you there.

Hotel Radisson SAS
390, Av. Marechal Craveiro Lopes, 1700
☎ 758 67 87
➠ 758 69 49
● *Esc. 25,000*

The following hotels are also located within a a short taxi ride from the airport:

Roma ➠ 28
33, Av. de Roma, 1700
☎ 793 29 74
➠ 793 29 81
● *Esc. 11,500*

Lutécia
52, Av. Frei Miguel Contreiras, 1700
☎ 849 70 11
➠ 840 78 18
● *Esc. 14,500*

Penta
Av. dos Combatentes, 1600
☎ 726 40 54
➠ 726 99 74
● *Esc. 15,200*

Car rental

Several agencies have their offices near the exit from the arrival terminal, and this is the best place to rent from if you are driving outside Lisbon.
◷ *open daily 6–1 am*

Autojardim
☎ 846 31 87
➠ 846 31 77

Hertz
☎ 849 27 22
➠ 840 14 96

Avis
☎ 849 48 36
➠ 846 31 70

Europcar
☎ 840 11 63
➠ 846 31 77

Basic facts

Lisbon has good train connections with France and Spain. The quickest way to travel to Lisbon from Paris (the total trip takes about 20 hours) is by TGV south and change at Irun on the Spanish border. From Madrid, the most direct trains leave Atocha station and take 6–10 hours.

➡ Getting there

By train

Santa Apolónia station

Long-distance trains from Paris, Madrid, Coïmbra, Porto and the north of Portugal all stop at Santa Apolónia station, which is at the foot of the Alfama district on Avenida Infante Dom Henrique. The station is a short walk from the city center. It is also well served by buses and there is a taxi stand outside the main entrance. Inside the station you can get tourist information and advice about accommodation from the Posto de Turismo (open Mon.–Sat. 9am–7pm). You can also change money at the station's currency-exchange office.

Information
☎ 888 40 25
🕐 open daily 8am–10pm

Lost property
☎ 881 61 11
🕐 Mon.–Fri. 9am–6pm

Left luggage
Gate 47

Car rental
Gate 47
Europcar
☎ 886 15 73
➡ 886 15 73
🕐 Mon.–Fri. 8am–8pm
Avis
☎ 881 04 69
🕐 daily 8.30am–1pm, 3–9pm

Other stations

Rossio station
Rossio station in Praça dos Restauradores serves Queluz (about 20 minutes away), Sintra (45 minutes away), Amadora and the Estremadura coast as far as Figueira da Foz.

Cais do Sodré station
From Cais do Sodre station on Avenida 24 de Julho, trains depart for Estoril, Cascais and the West.

Terreiro do Paço station
Terreiro do Paco station on Praça do Comércio serves the Algarve, Seville and Alentejo and Barreiro regions.

Leaving Lisbon by train
Leave Lisbon at 5.03pm, arrive in Hendaye at 9am. *Leave on TGV Atlantique 9.37am arrive in Paris at 2.55pm.*
● *Single ticket Esc. 24 500*

By bus

There is a service to Lisbon once a week. You can buy tickets in Britain from a Eurolines or National Express agent, or from Victoria Coach Station in London.

If you make your own way to Paris, there are buses every day in high season (July 2–September 10) and five days a week (Tue., Thur.–Sun.) in low season.
In Paris, buses for Lisbon depart from Gallieni bus station, at 28, Av.

du Général-de-Gaulle.
M Gallieni
In low season, buses leave at 2pm and arrive the following day at 1.45pm.
● *A round-trip from London costs roughly £130 or $210. From Paris it costs around £90 or $145 in low season; add on another £10 or $15 each way in high season. Lisbon's main bus station, the Rodoviária Nacional, is located on Avenida Casal Ribeiro, 1200. It is near the center and has good transportation connections as well as a taxi stand.*

Leaving Lisbon by bus
To book a bus ticket to leave

Lisbon for destinations in Spain or France, you'll need to contact the Portuguese Eurolines agency, *55, Rua Actor Toborda, 1050* ☎ *354 73 00* ⊙ *Mon.–Fri. 8am–7pm Departures are from the bus station, Rodoviária Nacional 18, Av. Casal Ribeiro, 1200* ☎ *354 54 39*

By car
Lisbon is joined to the rest of the country by five expressways: the A1, A2, A5, A8 and A9. All are toll roads. If you're coming from the north over the Spanish border, you will pay around Esc. 2500 in tolls. The A1 is

the usual route from Porto and the north. The A5 brings traffic from Cascais and the coast, while the A8 is the route from Torres Vedras and the coastal region. If you're coming from the south or east, for instance from Madrid, the standard route is the A2 via the Ponte 25 de Abril. The recently opened Vasco da Gama bridge to the northeast of the city links the north of Lisbon with Montijo on the south side of the Tagus.

You can also enter the city by ferry across the river: car ferries operate day and night between the north and the south side of the

Tagus. Crossings on the south side are from Montijo, Barreiro and Almada.

Although driving in Portugal is a wonderful way to see the country, roads apart from the expressways are poor. Using a car in Lisbon itself can often be more of a liability than an advantage. Street parking is difficult, so if you do bring a car to the city, look for off-street parking facilities.

Breakdowns
If you break down, call out the ***Automóvel Clube de Portugal*** *Rua da Guiné, Prior Velho, 2685 Sacavém* ☎ *942 91 03* ⊙ *24-hour service*

Basic facts

Lisbon's varieties of transportation contribute to its unique charm. The old-style streetcars and the more modern ones are a pleasant way to explore the charming historical districts. The city also has three funiculars and an elevator, the Elevador de Santa Justa, not to mention

Getting around

Carris

The streetcars, funiculars and buses are all run by the state-owned company, Carris. You can buy tickets from Carris kiosks, located in the main squares.

Tickets

BUC (módulos)
● *A ticket valid for two trips on all Carris transport, can be bought from a kiosk in advance and costs Esc.150. Tickets bought on the bus also cost Esc.150 but are only valid for a single trip.*
Passe turístico
Travel passes are available at kiosks and are valid on buses, funiculars, streetcars, the elevator and subway.
● *One-day pass: Esc. 430; 3-day pass: Esc. 1000; 4-day pass: Esc. 1600; 7-day pass: Esc. 2265*

Information

☎ *363 20 44*

Lisboa Card

The Lisboa Card allows you to travel freely on the subway and other Carris transportation and gives you free entry to 25 major city museums and those just outside as well as a reduction of between 10 and 30% on other attractions.
The card can be bought at 50 Rua Jardim do Regedor, Mosteiro dos Jerónimos and the Museu Nacional de Arte Antiga.
● *A card valid for 24 hours costs Esc. 1500, a 48-hour card costs Esc. 2500, and a 72-hour card is Esc. 3250.*

Buses

Buses run fairly frequently and are ideal for getting to outlying areas.

At each stop (*paragem*), you'll find information about the route, schedules and night-buses. Bus maps are on sale at Carris kiosks.

Streetcars

The old-style streetcars (*eléctricos*) still rattle up Lisbon's impossibly steep gradients. The most popular line is route 28 which traverses the picturesque districts of Alfama, Graça, Bairro Alto and Estrela. It is the most practical way to get up to Castelo São Jorge ➡ 90 and the Feira da Ladra ➡ 94 ➡ 146. The ultra-modern number 15 streetcar follows a route along the Tagus to Belém.

Eléctrico de Turismo

Sightseeing tours in red streetcars

or yellow double-decker buses start from the Praça do Comércio. Two tours are offered: one takes you around the Alfama and the Bairro Alto (Linha das Colinhas), the other (Linha do Tejo) is a tour of the banks of the Tagus.

The funiculars and elevators

The funiculars provide amazing views over the city and often stop at panoramic viewpoints (*miradouros*). The Elevador da Glória is a quick and easy way of getting from the Praça dos Restauradores up to the Bairro Alto.
🕐 *daily 7–12.30am*
The other two funiculars are the Elevador da Bica,

buses, a subway, and *caciheiros* (ferries), which ply the Tagus.

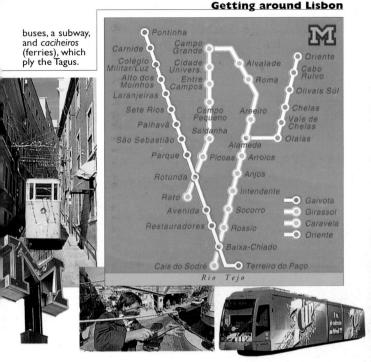

which links Rua de São Paulo with Largo Calhariz and the Elevador do Lavra, which links Largo da Anunciação with Rua Câmara Pestana. The Elevador de Santa Justa is a sort of street elevator and provides great views over the Baixa and Castelo São Jorge ➡ 90. At the top a walkway leads to the Chiado.
🕐 *Mon.–Sat. 7am–11pm; Sun. 9am–11pm*

Subway

Lisbon's subway is among the cleanest, slickest and fastest in Europe. Two lines, running north to south, link the city's important sites. Extensions are under way in the Chiado, the Baixa and the Rato and a line is also being extended as far

as Cais do Sodré. Buy tickets at the stations.
● *One-way ticket: Esc. 70; book of ten tickets (caderneta): Esc. 550; day pass: Esc. 200; 7-day pass: Esc. 620.*
🕐 *6.30–1am*

Information
☎ *355 84 57*
🕐 *9am–1pm, 2.30–5pm*

Ferries

Ferries run by Transtejo link the city with the south side of the Tagus and are worth taking for the wonderful views of Lisbon. Ferries from Cais do Sodré take foot passengers and cars.
🕐 *5am–10pm, departures every 15 mins. 10pm–2.30am, departures every 30–40 mins.* Ferries from Praça do Comércio take

foot passengers only.
🕐 *daily departures 6am–9.30pm every 15 mins.*
● *Esc. 90 per person, Esc. 200 per car*
☎ *882 03 61*
Ferries also cross from Belém to Trafaria, where you can catch buses to the beaches at Caparica.
🕐 *daily departures 7am–9pm*

Sightseeing trips

Mini-cruises last two hours and are an ideal way to see Lisbon from the river. They operate from April 1 to October 31.
🕐 *11am, 3pm*
● *Esc. 3000*
☎ *882 03 48*

Taxis

Taxis are fairly inexpensive. You'll find taxi stands in the main squares or you can flag

one down in the street. A green light means the taxi is occupied.
● *The minimum charge is Esc. 250. An average ride within the city limits costs Esc. 500. At night, (10pm–6am), on Saturdays, Sundays and public holidays the fare is a little more. Taxi-drivers accept cash only. Meters indicate the fare and it is usual to add a tip of 10%.*
Teletaxis
🕐 *24 hours*
☎ *811 11 00*
➡ *815 17 90*

Driving

Driving in Lisbon is not recommended as the streets are narrow, there are many one-way streets and parking is difficult. But a car is useful for trips outside the city, as it gives an independence public services cannot provide.

Most stores are open from Monday to Friday 9am–1pm and from 3pm to around 7pm. They are closed on Saturday afternoons, Sundays and public holidays. Note that banks are closed all day Saturday and Sunday.

Getting by

Money

Cash can be obtained using a credit card with a PIN number from the numerous Multibanco cash dispensers. They accept most international credit and debit cards. Major credit cards are also accepted at most restaurants, hotels and stores.

Currency

The unit of currency is the escudo (Esc. or $), divided into 100 centavos. Notes come in denominations of Esc. 500, 1000, 2000, 5000 and 10,000.

Exchange rate

Esc. 190 = about $1; Esc. 300 = about £1. Many banks have currency exchange desks with fixed commission rates.

Currency exchange offices can be found in the main squares and there is a 24-hour service at the airport.

Tipping

This is not obligatory as service is always included in the price. But it is usual to give a 10% tip to taxi-drivers and waiters.

Media

Portuguese newspapers

Main daily papers are the *Público*, *Diário de Notícias* and *Jornal de Notícias*. The weeklies are *O Expresso* and *O Independente*. On Sundays, the *Diário de Notícias* comes with the *Agenda Cultural* supplement, which has listings of shows and cultural events.

International newspapers

You can buy most international newspapers, weeklies and magazines at *Distri Lojas* Amoreiras Shopping Center or at the *Tabacaria Britânica* Cais do Sodré English-language newspapers that are printed in Europe can be bought on the day of publication. Other publications usually arrive a day later. The weekly *Anglo-Portuguese News* is the principal English-language publication in Lisbon, and is mainly for the British expatriate community.

Television

For a long time Portugal had only two television channels: RTP 1 and RTP 2, which were started under Salazar. But since 1992, the privately owned SIC has been offering a wide choice of programs and has built up good audience ratings. Most movies are broadcast in the original language with Portuguese subtitles. *Telenovelas* (soap operas) have a specially devoted following!

Tourist information office (1)

Palácio Foz
Praça dos Restauradores,
1200
☎ 346 33 14
🕐 open daily 9am–8pm

Lost property

180, Praça Cidade de Salazar,
1800 Olivais
☎ 853 54 03

◷ *Mon.–Fri. 9.30am–12.30pm, 1.30–5pm* Carris has a lost property office at the top of the Santa Justa elevator ➤ 12.

Telephones

The area code for Lisbon and surrounding areas, including Sintra, Cascais and Estoril, is (01). The code for Óbidos is 062 and for Mafra 061. Always dial the area code if you are calling from one area to another, but within the same area dial only the 7-figure number.

Telephone codes

To phone abroad from Lisbon you must first dial 00 and then the country code. The country code for the USA and Canada is 1, the UK is 44,

Australia 61, New Zealand 64 and Ireland 353. Next dial the area code minus the initial zero and then the number. To phone Lisbon from abroad phone 00 35 11 and then the local number.

Operator connections

Directory enquiries ☎ 118 International directory enquiries ☎ 098 To call collect: *within Portugal* ☎ 118 *to Europe* ☎ 099 *to other countries* ☎ 098

Public phones

There are both pay phones and card phones in Lisbon. Phone cards are on sale in post offices, at some news stands, and in stores showing a *Cartões de telefone* sign. You cannot

receive calls from abroad on any public phone, but you can call abroad from most telephones and from the telephone exchange **(2)** at 68, Praça do Rossio. *Planet Cópias e Imagem* 41-B, Av. da República, 1200 ◷ *open daily 24 hours except Jan. 1, Easter and Dec 25.* For sending or receiving faxes.

Internet

Web Café **(3)** 12, Rua do Diário de Notícias, 1200 ◷ *open daily 2pm–2am* @ *web1@mail.eso terica.pt* For surfing the net and checking your electronic mail ➤ 65.

Mail **(4)**

Post offices

◷ *Mon.–Fri. 9am–6pm; Sat.*

9am–1pm
Main post office
58, Praça dos Restauradores 1200
◷ *open daily 8am–midnight*

Emergency numbers

Police
☎ 346 61 41

General emergencies
☎ 112

Fire department
☎ 342 22 22

Hospitals
◷ *24 hours*
Hospital São José
Rua José António Serrano, 1150
☎ 886 01 31
Hospital Santa Maria
Av. Professor Egas Moniz, 1600
☎ 797 51 71

Alcohol

The sale of alcohol is forbidden to anyone under the age of 21.

A reservation is recommended during the high season (Easter, summer, fairs, exhibitions). Note that prices may rise significantly during any festival or special event (such as Expo '98).

► Where to stay

Price range

The following information is given for each hotel: the number of rooms, the price range for a double room, the number of suites and their starting price, the price for the cheapest breakfast available. The price of a room is often negotiable depending on the length of your stay, the season and the number of people. This applies particularly to pensions ➠ 18.

47
Hotels
THE INSIDER'S FAVORITES

Including pensions, hostels and apartments

Pensões

In some of these old family pensions it is still possible to rent a room for the whole year! The service is basic but adequate. For those on a tight budget, a double room costs less than Esc. 10,000 or £30/$48 ➠ 18.

Hotel apartments

These hotels offer apartments with kitchenettes or full kitchens.
Orion Eden ➠ 20
Dom Rodrigo ➠ 24
Meliá Confort ➠ 26

Youth hostels

There is only one in Lisbon. Guests can register at any time of the night or day on presentation of a national or international youth hostel card.
46, Rua Andrade Corvo, 1050
☎ 353 26 96.
For reservations, call MOVIJOVEM
☎ 313 88 20 ➠ 352 86 21
Double room: Esc. 4500
Dormitory: Esc. 1900

The traditional *pensão* was often full of guests who stayed the whole year, almost as part of the family. Today the *pensãos* are as welcoming as ever, even if they have lost a little of this atmosphere. They offer a basic but adequate service, usually at a reasonable price (less than £35 a night for a double room). They are also usually well-situated in the center of town.

Where to stay

Pensão Ninho das Águias (1)

74, Rua Costa do Castelo, 1100
☎ 886 70 08
Ⓜ Socorro
16 rooms ●
📁 📷 ⌗

Built up against the walls of the Castelo São Jorge ➡ 90, this small pension is surrounded by beautifully lush vegetation. Basic rooms are available with or without a bathroom. ★ From the terrace on the top floor, there is an unparalleled view over the city. Reservations are highly recommended.

Casa de São Mamede (2)

159, Rua da Escola Politécnica, 1250
☎ 396 31 66
➡ 395 18 96
Ⓜ Rotunda
28 rooms ●●
📁 🎵 *Esc. 600*
📷 🖥

Situated opposite the Igreja de São Mamede and very close to the Jardim Botânico ➡ 110, this was one of the first buildings to be constructed after the severe earthquake of 1755. The rooms vary in size but are all 1950s in both style and decoration. Beautiful *azulejos* adorn the dining room.

Pensão Imperial (3)

78, Praça dos Restauradores, 1250
☎ 342 01 66
Ⓜ Restauradores
17 rooms ●
📁 📷 ⌗

The reception desk of this pension is found up five flights of stairs at the back of a store specializing in the occult! The most comfortable rooms (with bathroom) are on this floor. ★ Attic rooms on the 6th floor are slightly less expensive and give a view across the city's rooftops. The staff speak English, French, and Portuguese.

Pensão João da Praça (4)

97, Rua João da Praça, 1100
☎ 886 25 91
or 886 13 78
➡ 886 25 91
Ⓜ Rossio
18 rooms ●
📁 📷 🖥 ⌗

A pleasant pension built on the hillside directly behind the Sé Cathedral ➡ 92, in the middle of the typical Alfama district, one of the typical areas of Lisbon. The rooms are spacious and available with or without bathroom. ★ Those on the top floor have good views over the Tagus and the Alfama district.

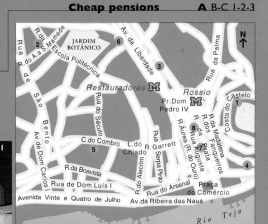

Residencial Santa Catarina (5)

6, Rua Dr Luis de Almeida e Albuquerque, 1200
☎ 346 61 06
➡ 347 72 27
Ⓜ Rossio, Chiado
18 rooms ●
▣ ⌂ ▣

This small pension is quiet and simple with all modern comforts. It is located in a narrow street lined with white limestone façades typical of the Bairro Alto. The large rooms are well maintained. The Chiado district, with its many bars and restaurants, is close by.

Residencial Roma (6)

22a, Travessa da Glória, 1250
☎ 346 05 57
➡ 346 05 57
Ⓜ Restauradores
24 rooms ●
▣ ⌂ ▣

A charming 1970s atmosphere awaits you inside this small pension, that is somewhat obscured behind a run-down façade. All the bedrooms are large and comfortable and the location is very central, close to the Avenida da Liberdade and a convenient stone's throw away from the Praça dos Restauradores.

Pensão Duas Nações (7)

41, Rua da Vitória, 1100
☎ 346 07 10
➡ 347 02 06
Ⓜ Restauradores
66 rooms ●
⌂ ▣ ⌖

Situated in the heart of Baixa, this charming little pension is run by the Borges hotel ➡ 20, which is one of the oldest establishments in Lisbon. The decor is simple and tasteful. ★ An attractive elevator takes you to the upper floors from where you have a wonderful view over the Baixa district.

Albergaria Insulana (8)

52, Rua da Assunção, 1100
☎ 342 31 31
Ⓜ Rossio
32 rooms ●
▣ ⌂ ▣ ⌖

Opened in 1972, this quiet and pleasant pension is situated in the heart of Baixa between two pedestrianized streets. On the 3rd floor you will find reception and a friendly lounge bar reminiscent of a gentleman's club. The rooms are simple and very attractively furnished, and some have a view over the Castelo São Jorge ➡ 90.

In the area

From Baixa trams, cable cars and elevators will take you from the lower part of the city to the upper part. ■ Where to eat ➡ 34 ➡ 35 ➡ 36 ➡ 41 ■ After dark ➡ 64 ➡ 66 ➡ 70 ➡ 76 ■ What to see ➡ 84 ➡ 86 ➡ 88 ➡ 90 ■ Where to shop ➡ 130 ➡ 132 ➡ 134 ➡ 136 ➡ 138 ➡ 142

Where to stay

Avenida Palace (9)
123, rua 1º de Dezembro, 1200 ☎ 346 01 51 ➡ 342 28 84

Ⓜ Restauradores Ⓟ **87 rooms** ●●●● 22 suites Esc. 40,000 ▭ ⓞ ▭ ☎ ▯ ▥ ⍦ ⍳ ✜

The Avenida Palace, which opened at the end of the 19th century, is a fine example of the luxury hotels available in Lisbon. Recent renovations have done nothing to detract from its *belle époque* charm; luxurious lounges decorated with buckskin and velvet, crystal chandeliers, stucco and a marble elevator all contribute to the sophisticated atmosphere of the surroundings. The rooms are chic and comfortable, and all are tastefully furnished in a classical style. The restaurant and bar are extremely welcoming. This is a centrally located hotel for those of refined tastes.

Hotel Métropole (10)
30, praça Dom Pedro IV, 1100
☎ 346 91 64 or 346 91 65 ➡ 346 91 66

Ⓜ Rossio Ⓟ **36 rooms** ●●● ▭ ⓞ ▭ ☎ ▥ ⍳ ✜

The Métropole is located in a handsome building on the edge of the large Rossio square. Renovated in 1993, the hotel made the most of its turn-of-the-century setting, giving its lounge and bar a 1920s look. The rooms are large and attractive and have been furnished with beautiful fabrics and furniture from the 1940s and 50s. ★ Some rooms overlook the rooftops of the old town and even have a small balcony from where you can just make out the Rossio.

Albergaria Senhora do Monte (11)
39, calçada do Monte, 1170
☎ 886 60 02 or 886 60 05 ➡ 887 77 83

Ⓜ Restauradores **28 rooms** ●●● ⍦ ⍫ ⓞ ▭ ☎ ▥ ⍳ ⌗

Built on a hillside in the district of Graça, this establishment doesn't look like much from the outside. However, behind the somewhat stark façade hides a charming hotel. ★ The rooms on the upper floors offer a wonderful view over old Lisbon. Furnished as they are in whitewood, the rooms are all extremely relaxing. Don't miss the chance of having your breakfast in the pretty courtyard bursting with plants, or trying out the panoramic restaurant upstairs.

Not forgetting

■ **Lisboa Tejo (12)** 4, poço do Borratém, 1100 ☎ 886 61 82 ➡ 886 51 63 ●● *Built in 1994, this attractive hotel is decorated with wood and azulejos and is tucked away in an old part of Lisbon.* ■ **Borges (13)** 108, rua Garrett, 1200 ☎ 346 19 51 ➡ 342 66 17 ● *Opened in 1885, this is one of the oldest hotels in Lisbon, ideally situated in the heart of the Chiado, close to the famous A Brasileira bar ➡ 64.* ■ **Orion Eden (14)** 18–24, praça dos Restauradores, 1250 ☎ 321 66 00 ➡ 321 66 66 ●● *Apartments and studios with kitchenette in an art deco building that used to house the Eden theater.* ■ **Hotel Mundial (15)** 4, rua Dom Duarte, 1100 ☎ 886 31 01 ➡ 887 91 29 ●●● *An 11-story tower in old Lisbon. Panoramic restaurant: Varanda de Lisboa ➡ 36.*

The imposing 1930s façade of the old Eden theater was very carefully preserved during the building of the Orion Eden hotel in 1996.

In the area

This imposing avenue stretches for over a mile toward the river. It was the first of the *avenidas novas* to be opened in 1880. Not far from here, however, is a small area known as the Parque Mayer which has escaped the clutches of the developers and was the home of theaters and opera

➡ Where to stay

Tivoli Lisboa (16)
185, avenida da Liberdade, 1250 ☎ 353 01 81 ➡ 357 94 61

Ⓜ *Avenida da Liberdade* Ⓟ 🏃 *327 rooms* ●●●●● *29 suites Esc.60,000* 🖤 *free to residents* ▯ Ⓞ ▭ ☎ 📠 Ⅲ 🍴 *Terraço Grill* Ⓨ *Zodiaco* 🃏 🗡 ✚ 🏊 🎾

Situated on the most famous avenue in the city, the Tivoli welcomes its guests into a peaceful and elegant setting. A top name in the Portuguese hotel industry since the 1950s, the Tivoli offers rooms that are both spacious and comfortable. On the top floor, the Terraço Grill offers both quality food and a spectacular view over the city. It is possible to dine outside in summer.

Lisboa Plaza (17)
7, travessa do Salitre, 1250 ☎ 346 39 22 ➡ 347 16 30

Ⓜ *Avenida da Liberdade* Ⓟ *112 rooms* ●●●● ▯ Ⓞ ▭ ☎ 📠 Ⅲ 🍴 *Quinta da Avenida* Ⓨ *Paddock* ✚

The Lisboa Plaza is situated in a quiet little street, far away from the noise and crowds. Once inside, you will find yourself in an elegant establishment where old and new furniture have been beautifully combined. Recently refurnished, the rooms have all been decorated in pastel shades and are extremely attractive. The simple and comfortable surroundings make you feel right at home. The bar is friendly and the restaurant (the Quinta da Avenida) has an excellent reputation for its Portuguese specialties.

Veneza (18)
189, avenida da Liberdade, 1250
☎ 352 26 18 or 352 67 00 ➡ 352 66 78

Ⓜ *Avenida da Liberdade, Rotunda* *37 rooms* ●● ▯ ▭ ☎ 📠 Ⅲ Ⓨ

A former Venetian palace that was transformed into an attractive hotel in 1990. The entrance hall, adorned with murals by Pedro Luís Gomes showing the districts of Lisbon, houses a magnificent marble staircase decorated with floral moldings. To reach the bedrooms, take the spiral staircase that eventually leads you to a beautiful open-work window. Verandas, stained-glass windows, and wrought ironwork complete the decor of this charming establishment.

In the area

■ **Tivoli Jardim (19)** 7, rua Júlio César Machado, 1250 ☎ 353 99 71 ➡ 355 65 66 ●●● *In an attractive setting with swimming pool and tennis courts.* ■ **Hotel Altis (20)** 11, rua Castilho, 1250 ☎ 314 24 96 or 314 42 06 ➡ 354 86 96 or 353 44 96 ●●●● *All the comforts of a 5-star hotel in a simple modern setting. Comfortable rooms and a fine view of the town from its restaurant, the Grill D. Fernando, on the top floor.* ■ **Hotel Britânia (21)** 17, rua Rodrigues Sampaio, 1150 ☎ 315 50 16 ➡ 315 50 21 ●● *Very large rooms in a 1940s building designed by Cassiano Branco. Renovated in 1995. Quiet location.* ■ **Sofitel (22)** 123–125, avenida da Liberdade, 1250 ☎ 342 92 02 ➡ 342 92 22 ●●●●● *A modern hotel opened in 1992. The piano bar and restaurant, opening out onto the avenue, are reminiscent of the belle époque.*

houses. ■ After dark ➡ 68
➡ 74 ➡ 78 ■ What to see
➡ 110 ■ Where to shop
➡ 140

22

17

17

16

19

18

The northern part of Lisbon has been taken over as business districts and São Sebastião is no exception. Today, this residential area is home to many banks and advertising agencies. All the same, it is quite close to the Parque Eduardo VII ➡ 110 and the Praça Marquês de Pombal.

➤ Where to stay

Ritz Lisboa (23)
88, rua Rodrigo da Fonseca, 1093 ☎ 383 20 20 ➡ 383 17 83

M Rotunda **P** *264 rooms* ●●●●● *20 suites Esc. 110,000* 🏠 ▢ ▣ 🖼 ⬛
▥ ⑂ *Varanda* 🟥 ▢ ◪ 🍽 ⊞ ✚ ♿

Built in the 1950s in the very heart of the city, the Ritz Lisboa has a reputation as one of the best hotels in Lisbon for the quality of its service. It has successfully combined the tradition of 19th-century palaces with the requirements of a modern and functional hotel. The recently renovated lobby contains impressive murals showing the districts of Lisbon. Its vast halls form a museum, housing works of art by the most important contemporary Portuguese artists (paintings, bas-reliefs, sculptures, ceramics, pottery, *azulejos*, and tapestries by Almada Negreiros). The large, comfortable rooms, tailored to modern needs, are furnished with great style. The suites all have impressive black marble bathrooms. Excellent lunchtime buffet in the Varanda restaurant.

Rex (24)
169, rua Castilho, 1070 ☎ 388 21 61 ➡ 388 75 81

M Rotunda *68 rooms* ●●● *9 suites Esc. 25,000* 🏠 ▢ ▣ 🖼 ⬛ ▥
⑂ *Cozinha d'El Rey* 🟥 *Clube 37* ✚ ⊻ *some rooms overlooking the park*

This well-situated hotel was completely remodeled in 1996 and now surprises its guests with its Austrian style of decor, complete with exposed beams and white walls. The rooms are small but comfortable. The restaurant, the Cozinha d'El Rey, is on two levels and has an attractive veranda. A buffet is served at lunchtime and an à la carte menu in the evening.

Amazónia (25)
12–20, travessa da Fabrica dos Pentes, 1200
☎ 387 70 06 ➡ 387 90 90

M Rotunda **P** *(charge for parking, – 50% for patrons) 192 rooms* ●●●
24 suites Esc. 22,000 🏠 *Esc. 1100* ▢ ▣ 🖼 ⬛ ▥ ⑂ *Vitória Régia* 🟥
Xingu 🍽 ✚ ≋ ✚ ♿ ⊻ *some rooms overlooking the Tagus*

Opened in 1990 in a quiet street, this relaxed hotel is decorated in an exotic style that recalls the Amazon, and is a favorite of traveling Brazilians. Its bar, overflowing with plants, is a tribute to the Xingu American Indian reserve.

Not forgetting

■ **Fénix (26)** 8, praça Marquês de Pombal, 1250 ☎ 386 21 21 ➡ 386 01 31 ●●●● *An unpretentious but expensive hotel that first opened in the early 1960s.* ■ **Dom Rodrigo (27)** 44, rua Rodrigo da Fonseca, 1250 ☎ 386 38 00 or 386 38 04 ➡ 386 30 00 ●●● *Studios and suites of rooms with fully equipped kitchens, decorated in a simple modern style.* ■ **Méridien Park Atlantic (28)** 149, rua Castilho, 1070 ☎ 383 09 00 or 383 04 00 ➡ 383 32 31 ●●●● *French hotel built in a modernist style. Rooms are small but comfortable.* ■ **Residencial Astória (29)** 10, rua Braancamp, 1297 ☎ 386 13 17 ➡ 386 04 91 ●● *An attractive 1920s-style hotel offering an inexpensive choice of accommodation.*

São Sebastião

R.P.Ant.Vieira
Rua Artilharia Um
R.Samp.   e Pina
Rua da Fonseca
Castilho
24
28
R.M.Subserra
PARQUE
EDUARDO VII
50
Rua Joaquim A.de Aguiar
23
Rua Rodrigo
da
Tr.F.D.Pentes
25
Rotunda II
Praça
Marquês
de Pombal
26
Rua
40
27
29
Rotunda I
Rua de S. Filipe Néry
Rua Braancamp
R.D.Palmela
Av. da
Liberdade
27

23
23
29
23
24
26

25

The monumental *avenidas novas* (new avenues) stretching north from the Praça Marquês Pombal, were built in the 19th century with little consideration given to practicality. Along the avenues are a few surviving buildings decorated with *azulejos* or the remains of others integrated

Where to stay

Executive Inn Hotel (30)
56, avenida Conde de Valbom, 1050 ☎ 795 11 57 ➡ 795 11 66

🅼 *São Sebastião* 🅿 *72 rooms* ●●● 🈺 ▭ ▣ 🈺 🛗 Ⅲ Ⅲ 🛡 ✚

This hotel is decorated in a contemporary style, with gray and white marble in the lobby, checked patterns for rugs and fabrics, and iron furniture in the bedrooms. The Executive Inn does not have its own restaurant, but breakfast can be taken in your room or outside in the adjoining garden in fine weather.

Marquês de Sá (31)
**130, avenida Miguel Bombarda, 1050
☎ 791 10 14 ➡ 793 69 83 or 793 69 86**

🅼 *São Sebastião* 🅿 🈺 *97 rooms* ●● 🈺 ▭ ▣ 🈺 🛗 Ⅲ 🍴 *Varanda do Marquês* 🛡 *Bar cocktail* ✚

Opened in 1996, the Marquês de Sá succeeds beautifully in combining modern design and traditional materials by using wood and black marble in the entrance hall and blue rugs and upholstery in the communal areas. All the rooms are comfortable and are decorated in pastel shades. The Varanda do Marquês restaurant offers diners both a large buffet and an à la carte menu.

Pensão Residencial Avenida Alameda (32)
4, avenida Sidónio Pais, 1050 ☎ 353 21 86 ➡ 352 67 03

🅼 *Parque, Rotunda* 🅿 *28 rooms* ●● 🈺 ▭ ▣ 🈺 Ⅲ (in 12 rooms) 🔆 *some rooms overlooking the park*

The entrance hall to this pension is also that of an apartment building, hence the mail boxes at reception. The place is quiet and friendly and simply furnished. Breakfast is served in the dining room on the top floor with views overlooking the Parque Eduardo VII ➡ 110.

Real Parque (33)
67, avenida Luis Bivar, 1050 ☎ 357 01 01 ➡ 357 07 50

🅼 *São Sebastião* 🅿 *153 rooms* ●●●●● *6 suites Esc. 45 000* 🈺 *Esc.1500* ▭ ▣ 🈺 🛗 Ⅲ 🍴 *Cozinha do Real* 🛡 *Do Real* 🏓 ✚ 🔆

Situated on the edge of the Parque Eduardo VII ➡ 110, the Real Parque offers friendly personal service. The modern practical decor is beautifully complemented by traditional woodwork and fabrics. ★ All rooms are spacious and comfortable and its café and restaurant overlook a small attractive garden.

Not forgetting
■ **Meliá Confort (34)** 45, avenida Duque de Loulé, 1050 ☎ 353 21 08 ➡ 353 18 65 ●●●● *Spacious apartments with kitchenette.*
■ **Miraparque (35)** 12, avenida Sidónio Pais, 1050 ☎ 352 42 86 ➡ 357 89 20 ●● *Pleasant hotel close to the Parque Eduardo VII ➡ 110.*
■ **Dom Carlos (36)** 121, avenida Duque de Loulé, 1050 ☎ 353 90 70 ➡ 352 07 28 ●● *Redecorated in 1995 reminiscent of the style of Lisbon hotels of the 1960s.*

into modern structures.
- After dark ➡ 74 ➡ 78
- What to see ➡ 98 ➡ 110
- Where to shop ➡ 130

31

36

35

32

In the area

While Campo Pequeno is now a booming business center, it still holds some cultural treasures. Opposite the bullring ➡ 100 stands the 18th-century Palacio Galveias which now houses the public library. ■ Where to eat ➡ 58 ■ After dark ➡ 74 ➡ 78 ■ What to see ➡ 98 ➡ 100

Where to stay

Barcelona (37)
10, rua Laura Alves, 1050 ☎ 795 42 75 ➡ 795 42 81

M *Campo Pequeno* P ☷ *125 rooms* ●●● *5 suites Esc. 29,000* ☷ *Esc. 1500* ☷ ☷ ☷ ☷ Ⅲ ☷ *Condal Bar* ☷ ☷ ☷ *views overlooking the Parque Monsanto* ➡ *108*

A modern hotel opened in 1992. The communal areas are furnished with comfortable sofas and decorated in a style that recalls the tapestries of José Guimares and Graça Morais. The rooms are subtly furnished with Italian-designed furniture and decorated in soothing shades of gray-blue. The restaurant is reserved for groups.

Quality (38)
7, Campo Grande, 1700 ☎ 795 75 55 ➡ 795 75 00

M *Entre Campos* P *83 rooms* ●●● *2 suites Esc. 35,000* ☷ ☷ ☷ ☷ ☷ Ⅲ ☷ *Café de Campo Grande* ☷ *Lobby Bar* ☷ ☷

Situated to the north of the city, near to Campo Grande (one of the new business districts), this establishment was opened in 1994 and welcomes its guests into pleasant surroundings. The rooms are comfortable and decorated in green and burgundy. Shades of beige have been chosen for the lobby, the bar, and the restaurant, adding to the relaxing atmosphere of the place.

Alif (39)
51, Campo Pequeno, 1000 ☎ 795 24 64 ➡ 795 41 16

M *Campo Pequeno* P *115 rooms* ●● *8 suites Esc. 22,500* ☷ *Esc. 1000* ☷ ☷ ☷ Ⅲ ☷ *Atlântico* ☷ *Bar Tejo* ☷

The modernist façade of this establishment hides a beautiful interior with strong Moorish influences. Walls, floors, and columns have all been covered with pink and beige marble. These light colors, combined with the profusion of house-plants, produce an extremely pleasant setting. In addition, there are a number of *azulejos* depicting the working-class areas of old Lisbon.

Not forgetting

■ **VIP Zurich (40)** 18, rua Ivone Silva, 1050 ☎ 793 71 11 or 793 72 07 ➡ 793 72 90 or 795 14 87 ●● *Built in 1990 in a quiet part of the city, the VIP Zurich offers comfortable rooms with light wood paneling.*
■ **Holiday Inn Lisboa (41)** 28-A, avenida António José de Almeida, 1000 ☎ 793 52 22 or 793 00 59 ➡ 795 23 04 or 793 66 72 ●●● *Large rooms and a good restaurant in an attractive setting close to the Avenida Republica.*
■ **Dom Afonso Henriques (42)** 8, rua Cristóvão Falcao, 1900 ☎ 614 65 74 ➡ 812 33 75 ●● *An unpretentious family hotel in a new district close to Expo '98.*
■ **Roma (43)** 33, avenida de Roma, 1700 ☎ 796 77 61 ➡ 793 29 81 ●● *Spacious rooms in a recently renovated modern hotel. Many movie theaters and stores in the area.*
■ **AS Lisboa (44)** 188, avenida Almirante Reis, 1000 ☎ 847 30 25 ➡ 847 30 34 ●● *A pleasant, comfortable hotel in a new part of town, on the way to Expo '98.*

Lapa is the smartest district of Lisbon, with magnificent residences set amid lush vegetation. The bars and discos of the Avenida 24 de Julho make this a lively district at night. ■ Where to eat ➡ 46 ■ After dark ➡ 72 ■ What to see ➡ 102

Where to stay

Hotel da Lapa (45)
4, rua Pau da Bandeira, 1200
☎ 395 00 05 or 395 00 06 ➡ 395 06 65

🔲 tram 25 🅿 🈺 *94 rooms* ●●●● *8 suites Esc. 65,000* 🈺 *Esc. 2350* ▬ ▭
☎ 🔟 🈺 🈺 🈺 *Embaixada* 🈺 *Rio Tejo* 🈺 🈺 🈺 🈺 🈺 🈺 🈺 🈺

The charming and stylish Hotel da Lapa opened in 1992. It is located in a town house dating from the end of the 19th century. In the entrance to this former mansion, the floor has been inlaid with marble, and the ceiling decorated with magnificent frescos. The hotel oozes luxury and comfort. The bedrooms are decorated in a wide range of different styles, from classical to 18th-century and art deco. All the rooms have marble bathrooms decorated with *azulejos*. ★ A number of rooms also have terraces which open onto a quiet garden that overlooks the Tagus. Sprinkled with waterfalls and fountains, this little garden with its lush vegetation is a paradise and is ideal for relaxing and unwinding after a hard day's sight-seeing.

York House (46)
32, rua das Janelas Verdes, 1200
☎ 396 24 35 or 396 27 85 ➡ 397 27 93

🔲 *14, 43, tram 15, 18* 🅿 *34 rooms* ●●●● 🈺 *Esc. 2000* ▬ ▭ ☎
🈺 *A Confraria* ➡ 46 🈺 🈺 🈺 *walled garden*

Behind an ivy-clad façade hides a wonderful establishment in which each lounge is more luxurious than the next. In the large bright rooms you will find beautiful four-poster beds. Antique furniture, ornaments, and Arraiolos rugs ➡ 140 complete the decor. The bar and restaurant ➡ 46 are equally attractive. ★ A stone staircase takes you to a small courtyard bursting with plants where you can enjoy tea or other meals in summer. This is really a wonderful haven of peace located in the very heart of the city, directly opposite the Museu de Arte Antiga Tapis d'Arraiolos ➡ 104.

As Janelas Verdes (47)
47, rua das Janelas Verdes, 1200 ☎ 396 81 43 ➡ 396 81 44

🔲 *14, 43, tram 15, tram 18* 🅿 🈺 *17 rooms* ●●● 🈺 *Esc. 1800* ▬ ▭ ☎
🔟 🈺 *My Bar* 🈺 🈺 *walled garden* 🈺 *some rooms overlooking the Tagus or the garden*

Located in an intimate, appealing setting in the same street as the York House, and slightly less expensive, is the Janelas Verdes. The hotel is housed in a building that is typical of 18th-century classical Portuguese architecture, and is said to be the former home of the most famous Portuguese novelist of the 19th century, Eça de Queirós. The overall atmosphere is very British, with antique ornaments and furniture from the colonies. The rooms are all equally charming; ★ and while those on the top floor are more basic, but they have a wonderful view over the Tagus. Breakfast can be taken in the small garden with its ivy-covered walls. While the hotel does not have its own restaurant, there are many to choose from in the area, as well as several discotheques that have opened on the docks ➡ 72.

Rua do Pau do Sacramento à Lapa
Rua da Bandeira
R. de São Félix
Rua R. das Praças
R. de S. João da Horta
Rua de S. Domingos
Rua Garcia da Mata
45
34
46 48
R.S.Fr. Porta
Rua da Arriaga
32
do Olival
47
Rua
Rua das Janelas Verdes
Rua do Prior
32
32
Avenida Vinte e Quatro de Julho
N
Rio Tejo

45

47

45

46

46

Where to eat

A taste of Lisbon cuisine

Lisbon's restaurants are highly influenced by traditional Portuguese dishes, paying tribute to the flavors and aromas of regional specialties and their rural roots. Whilst Lisbon was once described by the 14th-century chronicler Ferrão Lopes as the meeting place for "people from far and wide", foreign restaurants are few and far between.

Finding somewhere cheap to eat

There are many reasonably priced small restaurants ➡ 34 in Rua dos Correeiros, the Bairro Alto district, Rua da Madalena and Rua dos Bacalhoeiros, and in the narrow streets and alleyways of Pombaline Lisbon or in the even older districts of Mouraria, Alfama, Castelo and Madragoa.

61
Restaurants

THE INSIDER'S FAVORITES

Lisbon specialties

Açorda: a thick soup made with bread, oil, garlic and coriander (with meat, fish or seafood)
Bifana: pork escalope on a slice of bread
Cachucho frit: a type of bream (a freshwater fish)
Carapauzinhos: sticklebacks
Cozido a portuguesa: Portuguese casserole
Isca de fígado: poor man's *foie gras* (given the name by a French actor playing in Lisbon at the end of the 19th century)

Feijoada: bean stew
Mariscos: seafood
Pastel de bacalhau: cod fritter
Peixinhos da horta: boiled green beans covered in batter and fried
Petingas de escabeche: marinated sardines
Petiscos: a selection of small dishes and appetizers
Pipis: chopped chicken giblets in a thick sauce in which to dunk bread
Sopas: soups (wide range)

Restaurants serving plain simple food are popular today in Lisbon. Whether you decide to eat in a small family-run restaurant or a former inn, you can be certain that everything you eat will have been bought fresh from the market that day. For Esc. 1500 you can enjoy a full meal of soup, bread, the dish of the day and a choice of drink.

➡ Where to eat

João do Grão (1)

222, rua dos Correeiros, 1100
☎ 342 47 57
Ⓜ Rossio
🚌 numerous ●●
🕐 daily noon–3pm, 6.30–10pm

One of Lisbon's most famous restaurants during the 1960s, noted for its dried cod fish specialties, including the *meia-desfeita*: a dish of flaked dried cod served with chickpeas and seasoned with olive oil and fresh herbs.

Adega Zé da Viola (2)

25–27, rua da Madalena, 1100
Ⓜ Rossio
🚌 numerous ●
🕐 Mon.–Sat. 9am–9pm

A good, simple working-class establishment where you can try appetizers that the EU would like to ban the Portuguese from eating, including *petingas* and *joaquizinhos fritos* (small fried fish). Beautiful *azulejos* grace the entrance.

Adega Triunfo (3)

129, rua dos Bacalhoeiros, 1100
☎ 886 98 40
Ⓜ Rossio
🚌 numerous ●
🕐 daily noon–4pm; 6.30–11pm; closed Sun. from Oct.–Feb.

An establishment where the most typical dishes include *feijoada à transmontana* (bean stew), *cozido à portuguesa* (casserole), and *costeleta de vitela churrasco* (veal grilled over a wood fire).

Bota Alta (4)

35–37, travessa da Queimada, 1200
☎ 342 79 59
🚌 58, 100, tram 28 ●● 🕐 Mon.– Fri. noon–2.30pm, 7–10.30pm; Sat. 7–10.30pm

Be prepared to line up to get in. In a rare moment of silence, you may be able to hear the sound of a *fado* being sung in the street outside. The works of art hanging on the walls are as vibrant as the restaurant itself.

Casa da Mó (5)

1, rua dos Condes de Monsanto, 1200
☎ 887 20 95
🈳 numerous ●●
🕐 daily noon–10.30pm

A haven of peace in the very heart of the city. Pictures of Lisbon at the turn of the century line the walls and the kitchen prepares good honest traditional dishes. You can admire the lobsters climbing over each other in the large tank.

Cervejaria Ruca (6)

47, rua da Conceição, 1100
☎ 887 94 33
🈳 numerous ●
🕐 Mon.–Fri. noon–9pm; Sat. noon–3.30pm

A charming restaurant where the most famous dish is dried cod with chickpeas cooked à la lagareiro (in the oven with olive oil, milk, and potatoes). The king prawns in garlic are also a must. Very fast service!

Alfaia (7)

18–24, travessa da Queimada, 1200
☎ 346 12 32
🈳 100, 58, tram 28 ● 🕐 daily noon–3.30pm, 7–11.30pm

Currently very fashionable, this old establishment is popular with those living and working in the Bairro Alto. In addition to traditional dishes, the menu includes a wide range of baked, grilled, or fried fresh fish. Lively atmosphere.

Adega Tagarro (8)

21, rua Luz Soriano, 1200 ☎ 346 46 20 🈳 tram 28 ●
🕐 Mon.–Sat. 7am–midnight

The Adega Tagarro is one of the most popular restaurants in the Bairro Alto and has many regulars. On the menu are fresh fish and meat to be cooked on the grill, or more substantial dishes such as dried cod, cozido (casserole), and feijoadas (bean stew).

35

Once the cultural center of Lisbon, this district has changed recently. Typical is pedestrianized Rua de Santo Antão, which is very animated at night. ■ Where to stay ➡ 18 ➡ 20 ■ After dark ➡ 64 ➡ 66 ➡ 76 ■ What to see ➡ 84 ➡ 86 ➡ 90 ■ Where to shop ➡ 132 ➡ 134

➡ Where to eat

Gambrinus (9)
23–25, rua das Portas de Santo Antão, 1150 ☎ 342 14 66 ➡ 346 50 32

Ⓜ *Rossio, Restauradores* 🚌 *numerous* ●●●●● ▭ 🕐 *daily noon–2am* 🍸

One of the most famous restaurants in Lisbon. The bistro (*cervejaria*) at the front offers a fine selection of roasted or grilled meat sandwiches, savory snacks, and seafood. In the two dining rooms, the service is impeccable while the food is sophisticated, full of flavor, and typical of that found in the north of Portugal and Galicia. The menu includes a thick fish soup (made entirely from sea fish), bass (*robalo*) à la minhota, and steamed partridge served with chestnuts. The desserts are typically Portuguese, that is to say, very sweet. The cellar is well stocked with Portuguese wines which are well looked after and served very professionally.

Varanda de Lisboa (10)
4, rua Dom Duarte, 1100 ☎ 886 31 01 ➡ 887 16 07

Ⓜ *Praça da Figueira* 🚌 *8, 43, 60, tram 17* ●●● 🕐 *daily noon–3.30pm, 7–11pm* 🍸 🍽

The restaurant of the Mundial is situated on the top floor of the Mundial hotel ➡ 20, and has splendid panoramic views over 'Pombaline Lisbon,' the Tagus, and the castle of São Jorge. The menu offers the usual hotel food, specializing in local dishes. On Thursdays, you are invited to enjoy a buffet of *pestiscos* (a selection of small dishes and appetizers). The cellar is famous for its red wines, including *Barca Velha*, a wine from the Douro valley in northen Portugal.

Verdemar (11)
142–144, rua das Portas de Santo Antão, 1150 ☎ 346 44 01

Ⓜ *Restauradores* 🚌 *numerous* ●●● 🕐 *Sun.–Fri. noon–3.30pm, 7–10.30pm*

A pleasant and popular restaurant attracting a friendly crowd, close to Praça dos Restauradores and Praça Rossio. The chef prepares a range of dishes from the Miño region (such as *bacalhau no forno à Narcisa e rojões*, baked cod served with minced pork) and a large selection of fresh fish and *mariscos* (seafood). Simple but beautifully prepared.

Via Graça (12)
9-B, rua Damasceno Monteiro, 1100 ☎ 887 08 30

Ⓜ *Socorro, tram 28* 🕐 *Mon.–Fri. 12.30–3.30pm, 5.30pm–12.30am; Sat. 5.30pm–12.30am* ●●●● 🍸 🍽

The Via Graça is situated in a large steel structure dating from the 1960s which seems to balance precariously on the hillside. From the dining room there is a breathtaking view over the oldest part of Lisbon. The kitchen is creative and uses only produce of the finest quality. Don't miss the fish, hare, and partridge soups, the pancakes filled with monkfish (*tamboril*) au gratin, the sole stuffed with prawns (*linguado com recheio de camarão*), the steak with Serra cheese, or the saddle of lamb with rosemary (*sela de borrego com molho de alecrim*). Finish off the meal with one of the wonderful pastries. Good selection of wines.

R. de São José
R. da Câmara
C. do Lavra
Pestana
R. do Inst.Bact.
R.do Desterro
C. do Desterro
Rua da Palma
Rua de São Lázaro
Benformoso
Rua da Bombarda
R.da S.do Monte
C.do Monte
R.da Damasceno Monteiro
R. das Olarias
Calçada do Monte
R. das Pórtias de St.Antão
Calçada de Santana
de Pena
Esc.
Socorro
R.do Terreirinho
Calçada de São
R. do A. da Graça
R.do Socorro
Rua da Palma
R. da Mouraria
R. dos Cavaleiros
C. de Santo André
C. da Graça
Largo da Graça
Av. da Liberdade
Praça dos Restauradores
Restauradores
ROSSIO
R.P. de Dezembro
R.B.Queiroz
Rossio
Praça Dom Pedro IV
Pr. da Figueira
Rua da Betesga
R. M. de Ponte de Lima
Pr. do Coleginho
Rua Costa do Castelo
CASTELO SÃO JORGE

From the top of the hills to the north of Baixa, you can enjoy the magnificent views over the busy, ever-changing Tagus.

➡ **Where to eat**

Muni (13)
117, rua dos Correeiros, 1100 ☎ 342 89 82

Ⓜ *Rossio* 🔲 *numerous* ●● ▭ 🕐 *Mon.–Fri. noon–4pm, 8pm–midnight, except public holidays*

Tucked away in one of the streets of 'Pombaline Lisbon,' an old vaulted tavern houses this small restaurant which specializes in *petiscos* (an assortment of small dishes and appetizers) and traditional Lisbon dishes: *carapaus e sardinhas de escabeche* (marinated stickleback and sardines), *pastéis de bacalhau* (fritters of cod), steak *à Marrare*, *iscas com elas* (slices of marinated cooked liver served with ham), and *cozido à portuguesa* (Portuguese casserole, served on Thursdays except in summer).

Dom Sopas (14)
48–50, rua da Madalena, 1100 ☎ 886 62 53 ➠ 886 73 51

Ⓜ *Rossio* 🔲 *numerous* ●● ▭ 🕐 *Mon.–Sat. noon–3pm, 8pm–midnight*

Still heavily influenced by traditional rural cuisine, Portugal is without a doubt the country in Europe that boasts the widest variety of soups and broths as regional specialties. ★ The menu at the recently opened Dom Sopas offers a large number of these which, following the rural tradition, are substantial enough to be a meal in themselves. These include shark, fish, and meat soups, the Dom Sopas soup, containing garlic and a specialty of Évora (the capital of the province of Alto Alentejo), and the *sopa seca que se agarra às costas* (literally: dry soup that clings to your back!). Also recommended is the rice with clams and fillets of fish, the black rice with cuttlefish (*chocos*), and the roast lamb.

Tágide (15)
18/20, largo da Academia Nacional das Belas Artes, 1200
☎ 342 07 20 ➠ 347 18 80

🔲 *numerous* ●●●●● ▭ 🕐 *Sun.–Fri. 12.30–2.30pm, 7.30–10.30pm* ● Ⓨ ⌘

Situated on the hills above Baixa, the Tágide takes its name from a nymph that is believed to live in the Tagus, and the restaurant itself has spectacular views over the river from the second floor. The decor of this former nightclub has been heavily influenced by the style of 18th-century houses in Lisbon, with numerous *azulejos* depicting Greek gods on the light-colored walls. The establishment is well worth a visit for its Portuguese and French menu. With a smart lounge for private meals on the first floor, this restaurant is highly recommended for business lunches and dinners.

Not forgetting

■ **Martinho da Arcada (16)** Arcadas do Terreiro do Paço, praça do Comércio, 1100 ☎ 886 62 13 ➠ 886 77 57 ●● 🕐 *Mon.–Sat. noon–3pm, 7–10pm Follow in the footsteps of Fernando Pessoa, author of* Maritime Ode, *who often came here for coffee; enjoy a meal in the restaurant which has retained its period atmosphere. Choose from* carne de porco à Alentejana *(a traditional dish from Alentejo),* bife à Martinho *(the house steak), or a range of fresh fish. The terrace under the arches has a wonderful view of the Tagus.*

■ Where to
shop ➡ 132
➡ 134 ➡ 136
➡ 142

14

CAFÉ RESTAURANTE
MARTINHO DA ARCADA

16

Restaurante

15

13

In the area

Take the No. 28 tram to discover Bairro Alto, a trendy district that attracts all types of artists. The slopes are literally packed with many bars and restaurants. ■ Where to stay ➡ 19 ➡ 20 ■ Where to eat ➡ 34 ➡ 35 ■ After dark ➡ 64 ➡ 66 ➡ 70 ➡ 72 ■ What to see

➡ Where to eat

Pap'Açorda (17)

57–59, rua da Atalaia, 1200
☎ 346 48 11
▣ 58, 100, tram 28 ●●●●
◐ Tue.–Sat. 12.30–2.30pm, 8–11.30pm; Mon. 8–11.30pm

An excellent new establishment in a recently restored tavern serves specialities from the regions with a few creative and modern touches. Try the açorda royale with lobster and king prawns (a thick soup made with bread and flavored with oil, garlic, and coriander), the fried goat with açorda, or the alcatra à moda de Terceira (rump steak from one of the nine islands of the Azores). Reservations are recommended for dinner.

À Vossa Mercê (18)

16, travessa das Mercês, 1200
☎ 346 73 45
▣ 100, 58, tram 28 ●● ◐ Mon.– Sat. noon–3pm, 7pm–midnight

A restaurant whose dishes are inspired by the Trasos-Montes (in the north) and Alentejo (in the south).
★ The menu offers a different dish each day of the week: braised cod and ham (presunto), asa de raie (skate wing), prepared using the chef's own recipe, and lebre (hare) with white beans, real cozido à portuguesa, polvo (rice with octopus) and roasted goat, cação (shark) in coriander, and rice with duck. You can also choose from perdix com castanhas (partridge with chestnuts), ham, and cooked meats (enchidos) from Trasos-Montes.

1° de Maio (19)

8, rua da Atalaia, 1200
☎ 342 68 40
▣ 100, 58, tram 28 ●● ◐ Mon.–Sat. noon–3pm, 7–10.30pm

This very popular restaurant – favored by journalists and artists who help to create an informal atmosphere – serves an excellent choice of deliciously plain fare made from the freshest produce. Try the fillets of peixe-gal with açorda (soup made with bread, oil, garlic, and coriander), cod and spicy rice fritters, and favas guisadas com enchidos (crushed beans and stuffing).

Casa Nostra (20)

60, travessa do Poço da Cidade, 1200 ☎ 342 59 31
▣ 100, 58, tram 28 ●●● ◐ Tue.–Fri. and

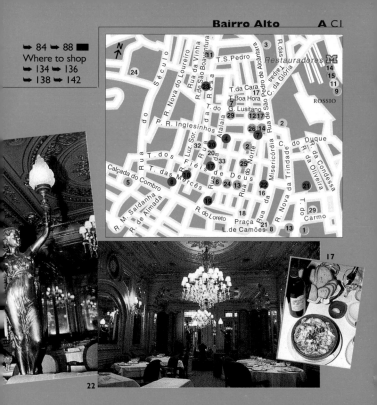

22

17

Sun. 12.30–
2.30pm, 8–11pm;
Sat. 8–11pm

The Casa
Nostra, with its
sophisticated
interior, is
situated in an old
house converted
to meet the
needs of a
restaurant.
It offers an
excellent menu
of Italian food:
Parma and San
Daniella ham,
Italian cooked
meats (enchidos),
sweet-and-sour
vegetables, snails
(caracóis) cooked
in tomato sauce
and mint,
sautéed
vegetables
(eirozes), fresh
pasta with
seafood,
escalopes in
Marsala, and
farrapos de carne
com míscaros e
limão (carpaccio).

Cervejaria Trindade (21)

20-C, rua da
Trindade, 1200
☎ 346 08 08
🚌 58, 100 ●●
🕐 daily
10am–2am

This huge café
is one of the
most popular
in Lisbon.
It is housed
in a former
monastery that
was turned into
a brewery before
it became a
café. The main
attractions are
the azulejos
depicting Masonic
motifs, and more
important, the
draft beer. The
main dishes on
offer are simple
appetizers, fresh
fish and seafood
of various kinds,
and fried cod
or steak.

Tavares Rico (22)

35–37, rua da
Misericórdia, 1200
☎ 342 11 12
🚌 58, 100, tram 28
●●●● 🕐
Mon.–Fri. 12.30–
3pm, 7.30–
10.30pm; Sun.
7.30–10.30pm

One of the
oldest and most
popular
restaurants in
Lisbon, Tavares
Rico is over a
hundred years
old. The menu
includes fillets of
sole (linguado) in
champagne,
lobster au gratin,
pato com laranja
ou estufado com
ananàs e foie gras
(duck in orange
or pineapple
with foie gras),
and iscas à Diogo
(slices of liver).
The self-service
restaurant on

the second floor
is quick and the
quality of the
food is excellent

El Gordo (23)

16-B, rua de São
Boaventura, 1200
☎ 342 42 66
🚌 58, 100 ●●●
🕐 Thur.–Tue.
5pm–2am

A place to enjoy
afternoon tea,
tapas (Spanish
appetizers),
dinner, or supper
beneath a ceiling
painted to
resemble a star-
studded sky. The
menu includes
French and
Portuguese
dishes. The
choice of wines
is judicious, the
atmosphere
pleasant, and the
service very
attentive.

In the area

Alfama and Mouraria, with their many steps and narrow streets, were once residential areas for sailors and fishermen who settled there after the 1755 earthquake. They remain the most authentic districts of the old city. Don't miss the fish market in Rua de São Pedro. ■ After dark ➡ 70

➡ Where to eat

Mercado Santa Clara (24)
Campo de Santa Clara, 1100 ☎ 887 39 86

▣ 12, tram 28 ●● ▭ ◐ *Tue.–Sat. noon–2.30pm, 7.30–10.30pm; Sun. noon–2.30pm*

This restaurant is situated on the top floor of the Santa Clara market building ➡ 146, one of the most beautiful structures of its kind in Lisbon. The dining room is small but very pleasant. The menu brings together some of the most typical dishes eaten in the capital, notably steak dishes traditionally served in the old bars and cafés. The selection includes steak *à Faustino, à Marrare, à Floresta, à Jansen*, and *à cortador*. Also available are *canjas de camarão* (clear shrimp soup), *ostras fingidas* (oysters), *bacalhau à brás* (cod served with small pieces of fried potato and eggs), *linguado rechaedo com camarão* (sole stuffed with shrimps), *assado de cordeiro no forno* (roast lamb, served on Saturdays), and *cozido à portuguesa* (Portuguese casserole, served at lunchtime on Sundays). If you are still hungry, or just have a rather sweet tooth, why not finish off your meal with one of the excellent desserts. The choice of wines is adequate and the staff are both friendly and helpful.

Lautasco (25)
7-A, beco do Azinhal, 1100 ☎ 886 01 73

▣ 9, 17, 35, 39, 46, 104, 105, tram 28 ●● ◐ *Mon.–Sat. noon–3pm, 7pm–midnight* ▣

This popular establishment, tucked away in the heart of the old affluent district of Alfama, serves Lisbon *petiscos* (a selection of small dishes and appetizers), as well as traditional Portuguese dishes. Fresh fish, served grilled or fried, is another specialty of Lautasco. The house wines are served in terracotta tumblers.

Parreirinha de Alfama (26)
1, beco do Espírito Santo, 1100 ☎ 886 82 09

▣ 9, 17, 35, 39, 46, 104, 105, tram 28 ●●●● ◐ *daily 4pm–2am* ♫ *Fados sung daily from 9.30pm*

Located in one of the narrow streets which typify the district of Alfama, this establishment is famous for the *fados*, the nostalgic songs that are Lisbon's traditional musical setting, which are sung in the evening every half an hour. Photographs of some of Portugal's most famous singers line the walls and testify to this tradition. The decor of the long room, complete with many *azulejos*, is typical of the *fado* houses that have become so popular with tourists. The menu is equally representative, offering regional specialties, all of which are of excellent quality and impeccably served. This is the perfect place to introduce your taste buds to the varied flavors of Lisbon and Portuguese cuisine! Those not wishing to eat a meal are welcome as long as they order a drink and some of the delicious appetizers. The Parreirinha de Alfama is only open in the late afternoon/evenings and, because this restaurant is very popular with locals as well as visitors, reservations are highly recommended. Friendly, bustling atmosphere.

The preserved Santa Clara market building retains its charm and is a fine example of an older architectural style.

43

In the area

As you walk around this area it will become clear that you are close to the political heart of the city. The National Assembly is here along with the official residence of the prime minister – which may explain why there are so many good restaurants in this district.

Where to eat

Casa Jervis (27)
107, rua de São Bento, 1200 ☎ 395 74 34

6, 49, tram 28 ●●● ▭ ○ *Mon.–Fri. 12.30–3pm, 7.30pm–midnight; Sat. 7.30pm–midnight*

You can't miss the entrance to this restaurant thanks to the Virginia creeper that completely covers the front of the building. An attractive little courtyard is available for those wishing to eat outside. The menu changes according to the season and is full of dishes that would once have been served by well-off Portuguese families. The result is mouth-watering: *coelho* (rabbit) *em molho São Cristóvão*, *codornizes* (quails) *de escabeche*, *bacalhau com molho podre* (cod in sauce), and *rabo de boi à nossa moda* (oxtail).

Conventual (28)
45, praça das Flores, 1200 ☎ 390 91 96 ➠ 390 92 46

100, tram 28 ●●●● ▭ ○ *Mon.–Fri. 12.30–3.30pm, 7.30–11pm; Sat. 7.30–11pm*

All that remains of this former convent is the statue of a saint watching over the tables of one of the city's finest restaurants: everything is first class, from the fittings and tasteful decoration to the service, the choice of wines, and, above all, the delicious food. The dishes, which are always imaginative, include *coxas de rã* (frogs' legs) from the monastery at Estremóz and *lombo linguado com molho de mariscos* (dab in seafood sauce).

XL (29)
57–63, calçada da Estrela, 1200 ☎ 395 61 18

6, 49, tram 28 ●●●● ▭ ○ *daily 8pm–2am* ▯

Currently very popular with those looking for a night on the town. It was originally famous for its steaks, but this reputation has now been extended to include fish baked in the oven and soufflés that are neither as soft or light as they should be, but nonetheless tasty. The menu also includes some interesting experiments with Japanese dishes. The wine list is adequate and the service efficient.

Café de São Bento (30)
212, rua de São Bento, 1200 ☎ 395 29 11

6, 49, tram 28 ●●● ▭ ○ *daily 6pm–2am* ▯

If, late at night, you get a sudden urge for a good steak and fries in a spicy sauce, then Café de São Bento is the place for you. It is quiet and friendly and the Serra da Estrela cheese, served with a final glass of red wine, is always a pleasure.

Not forgetting

■ **Rama Yana (31)** 2, rua Marcos de Portugal, 1200 ☎ 395 04 75 ●●● ○ *Mon.–Sat. 8pm–midnight One of the few exotic restaurants in Lisbon. Specialties from the East Indies: Malaysia and Indonesia. Don't miss the mesas de arroz (12 different rice dishes) and the cardamom cake.*

27

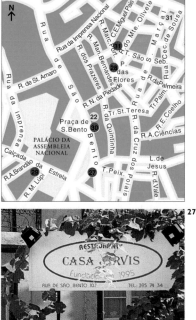

27

RESTAURANT
CASA JERVIS
Fundada em 1995
RUA DE SÃO BENTO 107   TEL.: 395 74 34

30

In the northwest of Rato lie the Mãe d'Água reservoir and the end of the Livres aqueduct which used to supply water to the whole city.

31

28

In the area

The two districts of Lapa and Madragoa may be next to each other but are very different in character. Lapa is aristocratic with a number of large houses, while Madragoa is lively and full of ordinary working people and has a large African community. ■ Where to stay ➡ 30

➡ Where to eat

Sua Excelência (32)
34–38, rua do Conde, 1200 ☎ 390 36 14 ➡ 396 75 85

▦ *13, 27, tram 25* ●●●● ▤ 🕐 *Mon., Tue., Thur., Fri. 1–3.30pm, 8–11.30pm; Sat. 8–11.30pm* 🍷

This tastefully renovated old establishment has a menu that brings together regional dishes from Portugal, Mozambique, and Angola: fish soup, Mozambique-style king prawns, Angolan moamba, steamed duck, and goat *chanfana* (a sort of fricassee). A further attraction is the owner, Francisco Queiros de Andrada, who recites the wine list in Portuguese, French, and English – to every newcomer.

York House-A Confraria (33)
32-1°, rua das Janelas Verdes, 1200 ☎ 396 24 35 or 396 81 43

▦ *13, 27, tram 25* ●●●● 🕐 *daily 12.30–3pm, 7–10pm* 🍷 🈯

The restaurant A Confraria, which is housed within the luxurious York House hotel ➡ 30, a former 17th-century monastery, cultivates an atmosphere of comfort and discretion. The talented chef, Eugénia Cerqueira, tempts diners each day with a range of tasty dishes including clam soup (*amêijoas*), baked cod with *broa* (corn bread), and roasted sheep's (*borrego*) feet in mint served with white beans. During the hunting season, a special menu includes such delicacies as partridge (*perdiz*), hare (*lebre*), and moorhen (*galinhola*). ★ Wine is available by the glass, which is unusual in Portuguese restaurants.

Nariz de Vinho Tinto (34)
75, rua do Conde, 1200 ☎ 395 30 35

▦ *13, 27, tram 25* ●●● 🕐 *Tue.–Sat. 12.30–3pm, 7.30pm–midnight*

The light room, large fans on the ceiling, and comfortable dark wooden chairs create a colonial atmosphere to complement the plain food made from only the finest produce: fresh fillets of fish served with rice, red beans, and the tops of *grelos* (turnips) or with *berbigão* (a shellfish similar to the clam). The wine list is small but of good quality; stick to red wines and port.

Not forgetting

■ **A Travessa (35)** 28, travessa das Inglesinhas, 1200 ☎ 390 20 34 ●●● 🕐 *Mon.–Fri. 12.30–4pm, 8pm–midnight; Sat. 8pm–midnight This establishment has a relaxed atmosphere and a mainly Belgian menu mixed with some French influences, and grilled fish dishes. On Saturday evenings, look out for five different mussel (mexilhões) dishes. Very good selection of Belgian beers. The menu also includes black pudding, Belgian sausage, stuffed eggplant, rabbit with prunes, steak tartare, and steak in a mustard sauce.*
■ **Café da Lapa (36)** 30–32, rua São João da Mata, 1200 ●●●● ☎ 396 26 83 🕐 *Tues.–Thurs., Sun. 8–11pm; Fri., Sat. 8pm–midnight The menu bears witness to the talent of Joaquim Figueiredo, a young Portuguese chef trained in France, and is guaranteed to please: cabrito assado em vinho branco e colorau (goat in white wine), pernil de porco glaceado em mel e tomilho ou outros (honey-glazed ham with thyme). The room is small but well laid-out.*

These *pastel de bacalhau*, cod fritters, are a Portuguese specialty: each restaurant has its own recipe.

This fortress-like shopping mall has drawn banks, advertising agencies, the media and other businesses to the surrounding area, shifting the city's business district. ■ Where to stay ➡ 24 ■ After dark ➡ 76 ■ What to see ➡ 102 ■ Where to shop ➡ 130 ➡ 140

➡ Where to eat

O Aviz das Amoreiras (37)
Amoreiras Shopping Center, loja 2058, 1200 ☎ 385 18 88

Ⓜ *Rotunda II* ●●●● ▣ Ⓞ *Mon.–Fri. 12.30–3.30pm, 7.30–11pm; Sat. 7.30–11pm* ⓨ ⊞ ⬛

Currently situated in the Amoreiras Shopping Center, the famous O Aviz restaurant will move back to the Chiado district, where it was originally opened in 1962, once the repair work has finished on buildings damaged in the fire of 1987. An interesting menu, tried and tested over many years, offers stuffed spider crab (*santola*), cod 'Count Guarda,' chicken Kiev, and lamb in mint sauce (*sela de cordeiro com molho de hotelão*). This large, luxurious, and tastefully decorated restaurant looks rather out of place in a modern shopping mall.

Coelho da Rocha (38)
104 A–B, rua Coelho da Rocha, 1200 ☎ 390 08 31

▣ *9, 74* ●●● ▣ Ⓞ *Mon.–Sat. noon–11pm; closed public holidays* ⓨ

Situated opposite the market, this restaurant offers good home cooking: *amêijoas* (clams) *à Bulhão Pato (a* 17th-century Portuguese writer and master chef), *açorda de mariscos* (seafood soup), *garoupa, cherne, goraz, dourada* (baked fish), *linguadinhos fritos com arroz de grelos* (small sole served with rice and vegetables), *arroz de cabidela* (rice with giblets), *arroz de coelho* (rice with rabbit), *borrego assado no forno* (roast lamb), and *empada de perdiz ou lebre* (partridge or hare pâté). The wine cellar is well-stocked and contains some good vintage Portuguese red wines.

Tasquinha d'Adelaide (39)
70–74, rua do Patrocínio, 1350 ☎ 396 22 39 ➡ 352 17 35

▣ *9, 74* ●●● ▣ Ⓞ *Mon.–Sat. 8.30pm–2am*

The ambience of this small restaurant is very unusual. Adelaide, the friendly head chef, has arranged the building so that the ovens are in the same room as the dining area. The design is actually that of her husband who is an architect. ★ You can dine well into the night on regional Portuguese dishes in a relaxed atmosphere that attracts the young particularly. Reservations are recommended as the dining area is small.

Not forgetting

■ **Casa da Comida (40)** 1, travessa das Amoreiras, 1250 ☎ 388 53 76 ➡ 387 51 32 ●●●●● Ⓞ *Mon.–Fri. 1–3pm, 8pm–midnight; Sat. 8pm–midnight One of the most expensive restaurants in Lisbon, its menu is polished rather than pretentious. Try, for example, the* casquinha de caranguejo *(stuffed crab), the* logosta com abacaxe *(lobster and avocado), the clam soup, the* pregado *(turbot) com pimenta verde, the partridge (perdiz) 'Convento de Alcântara,' the duck with ceps, or the four-pepper steak. Beautifully decorated room.*
■ **O Madeirense (41)** Amoreiras Shopping Center ☎ 381 31 40 ●●●● Ⓞ *daily 12.30–3.30pm, 7.30–10.30pm Regional dishes from Madeira, served in a setting that evokes the flora of the island's landscape. The menu offers traditional dishes such as black swordfish with banana (*filetes de peixe espada preto com banana*), tuna steak (atum) with fried corn, and aromatic beef kebobs on wooden skewers (*espetada de vaca em pau de loureiro*).*

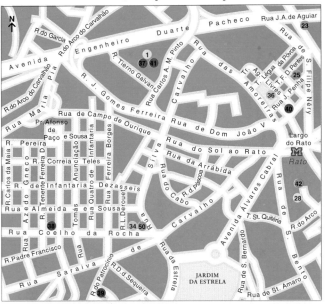

37

38

The Tasquinha d'Adelaide is in the heart of Campo de Ourique, a charming district with the atmosphere of a village.

39

For some time now the industrial district of Alcântara has been undergoing a transformation. As the inhabitants of Lisbon moved toward the docks, a number of architecturally adventurous buildings were erected between Baixa and Belém by well-known architects.

➡ Where to eat

Alcântara Café (42)
15, rua Maria Luísa Holstein, 1300
☎ 362 12 26 ➡ 362 29 48

🖼 Alcântara 🔲 numerous ●●●●● ▣ 🕐 daily 8pm–midnight 🅈
◉ Alcântara-Mar ➡ 72

The Alcântara Café has one of the most impressive dining rooms in the capital. The Portuguese architect António Pinto has pulled out all the stops to transform this former printing factory into a temple of design. The industrial architecture combines beautifully with the post-modern decor: steel girders, painted columns, and enormous fans. It is all just a case of getting accustomed to the unusual surroundings and lighting. The menu is equally innovative and unusual, but while the dishes are interesting, the quality can vary. Try, for example, the warm goat's cheese salad, the grilled fillet of hake (*cherne*) served with vegetables sautéed in garlic, or the duck flavored with rosemary. Gourmets will be unable to resist the imaginative pastries. The wine list is adequate and the service is friendly. ★ After dinner you can end the evening in the nearby disco, the Alcântara Mar ➡ 72, which is accessible via a metal walkway, or admire the works of art in the gallery. This address is currently very much in vogue with the fashionable set who come here as much to be seen as to enjoy the ambience, so be sure book your table well in advance.

Café-Café (43)
57, rua de Cascais, 1300 ☎ 361 03 10 ➡ 364 73 02

🖼 Alcântara 🔲 numerous ●●●● ▣ 🕐 Mon.–Sat. 8pm–1am 🅈 🅿
🎵 piano Wed.–Sat.

New to Lisbon, this ultra-modern restaurant, which was designed by the architects António Teixeira and Joaquim Proença, has begun to make a name for itself since one of the owners, the famous Portuguese political satirist Herman José, is often seen eating here. Diners can enjoy a cocktail on the first floor before making their way to the restaurant on the second floor, where the tables are arranged around a grand piano. The restaurant in the Café-Café is famous for its menu, created by Ricardo Carola, who is following in the tradition of his predecessor, Vitor Sobral. The latter is the leading light of the movement which has been termed 'Portuguese nouvelle cuisine' which, although not clearly defined, aims to refine a number of traditional Portuguese dishes and also improve their presentation. Typical recipes include seafood salads, such as *salada de endivias guarnecidas com puré de abacate e camarão* (endive salad with prawns and avocado purée), fish dishes, such as *sabores do mar com gengibre e tomato fresco* (a selection of fish in ginger and fresh tomato), *alcatra de peixe à moda do Pico* (an island in the Azores), and meat dishes, such as *vol-au-vent de aves selvagens* (fowl), and *tachinho de vitela em vinho d'Alhos* (veal cooked in wine from Alhos). The wine cellar is usually very well-stocked and the service is always friendly and obliging. The Café-Café has rapidly become the most fashionable place to eat in Lisbon and is a popular haunt of the Portuguese celebrities and socialites whose faces and activities provide such a rich and varied subject matter for the country's gossip magazines.

Alcântara **B** D1

42 **AL CANTARA** *café*
RESTAURANTE-BAR

Most of the restaurants around the docks have opened within the past two years since the Chamber of Deputies and Lisboans realized that the Tagus was one of the most exciting parts of the city. The restaurants in this fashionable area are always packed and no sooner have they finished serving meals than they reopen as bars.

➡ Where to eat

Doca de Santo Amaro (44)

🔼 Alcântara Mar 🚌 28
Doca 6 armazem 6 ☎ 395 79 05 ●●● 🕐 Tue.–Fri. 12.30–3pm, 7.30pm–midnight
Zonadoca pavilhão 7-A ☎ 397 20 10 ● 🕐 Wed.–Mon. 10.30–4.30am
Espalha Brasas armazem 12 ☎ 396 91 77 ●●● 🕐 daily 12.30pm–4am
Café in avenida Brasília, n° 311 ☎ 362 62 48 ●●●●● 🕐 daily 10am–4am
Zeno armazem 15 ☎ 397 39 51 ●● 🕐 Mon.–Sat. 12.30–4.30pm, 8pm–1.30am; Sun. 8pm–1.30am
Tertúlia do Tejo pavilhão 4 ☎ 395 55 52 ●●● 🕐 daily 12.30–3pm, 7.30–11pm
Doca de Santo ☎ 396 35 22 ● 🕐 daily 12.30pm–3am

Situated above the marina and in the shadow of the 25 de Abril bridge ➡ 112, Doca de Santo Amaro is the most famous of Lisbon's docks. On what resembles the bridge of a ship, patrons sitting on the terrace can watch the never-ending stream of boats going in and out of the port. Here families with various generations in tow, mix with clubbers decked out in their flashy evening wear. The Doca de Alcântara is set further back but this is where the larger restaurants and clubs are found. Two very different sets of people frequent this establishment: rich businessmen throwing their money around on a meal and a night out, and those without two cents to rub together who hang around until daybreak, making the most of what the night has to offer.

Rua da Cintura do Porto de Lisboa (45)

🔼 Cais do Sodre 🚌 numerous
Rock City Cais do Santos ☎ 342 86 36 ●● 🕐 summer daily 1pm–4am; winter daily 1–3.30pm, 8pm–4am
Docks ☎ n° 226, armazem H 395 08 56 ●●●● 🕐 daily 8.30pm–1am
Indochina n° 230, armazem H ☎ 395 58 75 ●●●● 🕐 daily 8.30pm–1.30am

Situated in the east of the city, beyond the Madre Deus and on the way to Expo '98, Doca do Poço do Bispo is as famous and popular as the other docks. The restaurants, which are mainly found in Rua da Cintura do Porto de Lisboa, are unusual in that they are all large complexes (with function rooms, restaurants and night clubs) into which the owners have invested heavily. The setting inevitably reflects the clientele: sophisticated establishments which attract a young and rich set who like to be seen.

Doca do Bom Sucesso (46)

🚌 29, 43, tram 15
Spazio Evasione avenida de Brasília, next to the Museu de Electricidade ☎ 362 42 32 ●●●● 🕐 Mon.–Sat. noon–3pm, 8pm–midnight
Vela Latina ☎ 301 71 18 ●●●●● 🕐 Mon.–Sat. 12.30–3pm, 8–11pm

In the cultural district of Belém ➡104 ➡106, the docks, once the scene of much maritime and industrial activity, have recently been converted into a small marina where luxury yachts and pleasure boats now mingle. Those frequenting the area differ from the other docks. Here you will mainly find people involved in local politics and finance. The highly fashionable restaurants bring together the jet set and visiting businessmen.

44

46

The most popular docks are at Poente (right bank), but with Expo '98 those at Nascente (left bank) should become just as popular.

44

46

44

In the area

The district of Belém acts as the cultural center with its large number of monuments, from the enormous Monastery to the National Coach Museum and the Palácio da Ajuda. Stroll along the riverbanks from where you can see the 25 de Abril bridge and the Cristo Rei.

➡ Where to eat

O Nobre (47)
71 A–B, rua das Mercês, 1300 ☎ 363 38 27 ➠ 362 38 27

14, 29, 32, tram 18 ●●●●● ▭ ◷ *Mon.–Fri. 12.30pm–1am; Sat. 7.30pm–1am* ▧ ▨

One of the finest Portuguese restaurants in Lisbon. The service is always particularly attentive (there is a doorman to park your car) and you can reserve one of the small rooms for your dinner party, a feature which sets it apart from other restaurants. The menu is creative and takes its inspiration from both Paris and Portugal. The fish and seafood are always meticulously prepared. Try, for example, the spider crab (*santola*) soup, or the small fillets of bass (*robalo*) à la Justa, named after the head chef. Meat dishes include roasted goat's (*cabrito*) feet, leg of duck in champagne, pork à la transmontana, and partridge from the Alcântara monastery. The cakes will appeal to gourmets and gourmands alike.

São Jerónimo (48)
12, rua dos Jerónimos, 1400 ☎ 364 87 96 ➠ 363 26 92

27, 28, 43, 49, 51, tram 15 ●●● ▭ ◷ *Mon.–Fri. 12.30–3pm, 7.30–10pm; Sat. 7.30–10pm* ▧

Ideally located on the road that runs along the side of the Mosteiro dos Jerónimos ➠ 106, this very attractive restaurant has a large bar and leather armchairs in the entrance, dimmed lighting, modern decor, and warm colors in the dining room. Like the setting, the menu is imaginative and polished: spider crab (*santola*) pancakes, artichokes (*alcachofras*) au gratin, *asa de raia com pêssegos* (skate wings in peaches), and duck (*pato*) in Muscatel and hazelnuts (*avelã*). To end the meal, choose from the selection of cakes displayed in the center of the room.

A Commenda (49)
Centro Cultural de Belém, 1400 ☎ 364 85 61

27, 28, 29, 49, tram 15 ●●● ▭ ◷ *Mon.–Fri. 12.30–3pm, 7.30–10.30pm; Sun. 11.30am–3pm* ▧ ▢ ▦

This restaurant is situated inside the modern Centro Cultural de Belém, one of the landmarks of contemporary Lisbon architecture. The menu is equally modern and is clearly influenced by the new trend in Portuguese cooking which aims to refine traditional dishes and make them less heavy. At lunchtime there is a buffet with a wide selection of hot and cold dishes. In the evening, the menu changes according to the season. Possible choices include *tamboril* (monkfish) *com azedas en creme de mostrada* (mustard), and *caracóis com molho de vinho verde* (snails in a vinho verde sauce).

Not forgetting

■ **Espelho d'Água (50)** avenida de Brasília, 1200 ☎ 301 73 73 ●●●● ◷ *Mon.–Fri. 12.30–3pm, 7.30–10.30pm; Sat. 7.30–10.30pm* Built on the banks of the Tagus in 1940, this glass building has wonderful views over the river, and on fine days, you can eat on the terrace. The menu is composed of regional dishes given an innovative twist: clams in vinaigrette, and lobster or partridge vol-au-vent to name but a few.

■ After dark ➡ 78
■ What to see ➡ 104
➡ 106 ➡ 110 ■ Where
to shop ➡ 144

49

Map labels:

Avenida da Ilha da Madeira
R. das Terras
R.das Pedreira
T.D.Tendeiro
T.da Memória
T. P. Martins   47
Rua Quinze
Av. do Restelo
R.Oito
Calçada do Galvão
da   Ajuda
Calçada   da
JARDIM DO ULTRAMAR
Rua Dom F. de Almeida
Rua dos Jerónimos
45
MOSTEIRO DOS JERÓNIMOS   46
51
43   44   42 Largo dos Jerónimos   37
R. de Belém   39
Praça Afonso de Albuquerque
Praça do Império
49 Fonte Luminosa
38   41
49
Avenida   da   Índia
N   40   50   38
Doca de Belém
Padrão dos Descobrimentos
Rio   Tejo

50

47

48

For some years the parkland of the Parque Florestal de Monsanto has provided green space for Lisboans. Recent attractions are the amusement park Parque Recreativo do Alto da Serafina and the Parque Ecológico. ■ Where to stay ➥ 30 ■ Where to eat ➥ 46 ➥ 48 ➥ 54 ■ After dark

➡ Where to eat

Tapadinha (51)
41-A, calçada da Tapada, 1300 ☎ 364 04 82

🔲 49, tram 18 ●● ▭ 🕑 Tue.–Sun. noon–3pm, 8pm–2am 🍴

When citizens of the states of the former Soviet Union were allowed to travel freely throughout the world, many Russians and Ukraininans, among other peoples of Eastern Europe came to the West to set up their own businesses. In Lisbon, a number of Russian restaurants have opened, of which Tapadinha is one. The walls of this simple place are covered with Soviet constructivist paintings and posters, some of which, by strange coincidence, resemble the 25 de Abril bridge ➥ 112 which rises above the restaurant. You can enjoy vodka, sturgeon and salmon caviar, and raw mackerel in a spicy sauce as well as bortsch, a broth containing five types of meat, steak tartare, ice creams, and pastries.

Papagaio da Serafina (52)
Parque Recreativo do Alto da Serafina, 1300 ☎ 774 28 88

🔲 2, 13 🅿 ●● ▭ 🕑 daily 12.30–3.30pm, 8–11pm 🍴 🍽 🌿

In spite of its size and the fact that it is made of glass and steel, this restaurant, which is in the heart of Lisbon's leafy suburbs at the entrance to the Parque do Alto da Serafina, manages to blend well into its surroundings. The internal decor, which is in keeping with the park outside, brings together wood and metal girders that are painted green. You will not be disappointed by the choice of the food either. For example: lobster *rissóis* (small pieces of pasta filled with lobster), *morcela da Beira na brasa* (braised black pudding), *sopa do mar* (seafood soup), *lombo de bacalhau com migas de pão de milho* (cod with corn bread), *panela de ferro com cozido de vitela e enchidos caseiros* (veal and the house selection of cooked meats), *cabrito à transmontana com arroz pingado de miúdos emborrachados* (lamb served with rice and giblets soaked in alcohol), and *lombo de vitela na telha com migas à moda da Beira* (veal). There is a very good selection of wines and the staff are friendly and helpful. This is the only restaurant to be found in the Parque Florestal, not far from the Aquedut ➥ 108.

Mercado do Peixe (53)
Estrada de Pedro Teixeira, 1400 ☎ 363 69 42 ⟶ 362 30 23

🔲 23, 29 🅿 ●●●●● ▭ 🕑 Tue.–Sat. noon–4pm, 7.30–11pm; Sun. noon–4pm

The Mercado do Peixe restaurant is situated in a former fish market, complete with the original stalls and the noisy atmosphere of a market. Here you are invited to try some of the freshest, and also most expensive, fish in Lisbon. Some of the fish are still alive, and are displayed in marble tanks and aquariums where diners may choose the one they wish to eat. The kitchen consists of a huge grill which is situated in the middle of the room where the fish is skillfully prepared and cooked in front of the diners. Those who enjoy eating meat should try the nearby Mercado do Carne restaurant, which opened in the former meat market in 1997. It offers suckling pig (*leitão*) and lamb (*cordeiro*) cooked over wood as well as barbecued beef, pork, and goat chops.

57

The tall modern towers of the new business district stand beside the 19th-century buildings of the *avenidas novas* and the few remaining monuments of old Lisbon — the Campo Pequeno bullring and the Palácio Galveias which now houses the National Library. ■ Where to stay ➡ 28

➡ Where to eat

Adega Tia Matilde (54)
77, rua da Beneficiência, 1000 ☎ 797 21 72 ➡ 793 90 00

🅼 *Praça de Espanha* 🔲 *31* 🅿 ●●●●● ◼ 🕐 *Mon.–Fri. noon–4.30pm, 7–11pm; Sat. noon–4.30pm* 🆈

Opened on May 1, 1926, the Adega Tia Matilde was just a local bar at that time. Today it is a comfortable restaurant that seats 130, although it retains the intimacy of its first days. It continues to serve Portuguese cuisine which is heavily influenced by rural recipes. Among the wide range of dishes to choose from are duck broth, puréed beans (*feijão*), clams (*amêijoas*), octopus (*polvo suado*), shad (*sável*, a fish similar to herring), and lamprey (*lampreia*, only available in season: March and April). Good selection of Portuguese wines.

● Funil (55)
82-A, avenida Elias Garcia, 1050 ☎ 796 60 77 ➡ 793 30 51

🅼 *Campo Pequeno* 🔲 *numerous* ●● ◼ 🕐 *Tue.–Sat. noon–3.30pm, 7–10.30pm; Sun. noon–3.30pm* 🆈

Situated in a shaded street, this restaurant is named after the only decorative object inside: a large copper funnel (*funil*). The clientele consists of the many regulars who come to enjoy the plain but delicious food. Whole families come to taste the restaurant's famous *bacalhau do Funil* (cod baked in the oven). Having eaten in the basement, diners often stop to chat on the first floor.

Isaura (56)
4B, avenida de Paris, 1000 ☎ 848 08 38 ➡ 848 66 51

🅼 *Areeiro* 🔲 *8, 40* ●● ◼ 🕐 *Sun.–Fri. noon–3.30pm, 7–11pm* 🆈

The main attraction of this establishment is its wide selection of Portuguese wines and the care with which they are looked after. From the menu, try *ovas fritas com arroz de mariscos* (fried fish eggs with rice and seafood), *cherne* (hake) or *tamboril à cataplana* (monkfish cooked in a copper pan traditionally used in the Algarve), *vitela* (veal) *assada à padeiro*, Marrare steak (a tribute to an Italian who ran one of the most famous cafés in Lisbon at the end of the 19th century), or *rancho* (a type of couscous with chickpeas) *à la Figueiró dos Vinhos*.

Kashmir (57)
15-B, rua Doutor Gama Barros, 1700 ☎ 849 41 13 ➡ 847 47 00

🅼 *Roma* 🔲 *7, 27, 33, 35, 67* ●● ◼ 🕐 *daily 12.30–3pm, 7.30pm–midnight* 🔲

An establishment where the atmosphere is spiced up with Indian specialties. In a quest to find the necessary flavors for their dishes, the Kashmir imports a lot of its produce. The menu includes such delicacies as *chamussas*, fried onions (*cebola*), *papari,* and *tandoori* made with fish and seafood: *garoupa* (a type of bream with white flesh), *salmonete* (mullet), *pescada* (whiting), and king prawns; and with meat: *frango* (chicken), *borrego* (lamb), and a mixture of meats. Vegetarian dishes, Indian cakes, and Darjeeling tea are also available.

■ After dark
➡ 74 ➡ 78
■ What to
see 98 ➡100

56

54

The Adega
Tia Matilde
restaurant is
just next to
the Gulbenkian
museum where
you can admire
the collections
of Portuguese
art ➡ 74 or
listen to a
concert ➡ 98.

55

There are a number of restaurants outside the city for those who like to venture further afield; enjoy a meal at the Quinta dos Frades on the way to Mafra ➡ 126; escape the crowds of the Centro Comercial Colombo ➡ 130 at the D'Avis; admire the views of the bridge and the Cristo Rei ➡ 112 from the Ponto Final on the opposite bank, or stop at the

➡ Where to eat

Quinta dos Frades (58)
5-D, rua Luís de Freitas Branco, 1600 ☎ 759 89 80 ➡ 758 67 18

🖼 7 (beside praça Chile), then 17 🅿 ●●● ⬛ 🕐 Mon.–Fri. noon–3.30pm, 7.30pm–midnight; Sat. noon–3.30pm 🍸

This light, modern, pleasant restaurant is situated in the Luminar, one of the outlying business development areas of the town, and is mainly frequented by businessmen. The menu varies according to the season and the produce available from the market. The chef concentrates on fresh fish and top-quality meat which is prepared simply under the grill. In warmer months, the menu includes a variety of salads made with lobster, roast beef, and *naco de novilho grelhado à hortelã* (grilled bullock with mint). In winter, these are replaced by rice dishes with fish and vegetables, *feijoadas* (bean stew), *cozido à portuguesa* (a Portuguese casserole made with several types of meat and served with vegetables and rice).

D'Avis (59)
96–98, rua do Grilo, 1900 ☎ 868 13 54 ➡ 868 13 54

Ⓜ Olaias 🖼 18, 39, 59 ●●● ⬛ 🕐 Mon.–Sat. noon–4pm, 7.30pm–midnight

In an atmosphere that is supposed to be sophisticated, but which is in reality wonderfully kitsch, you are invited to sample the richness of the dishes from Alto Alentejo: pig's tripe stuffed with flour, pig's ears in coriander, gaspacho, *açorda* (soup made with bread, oil, garlic, and coriander), *migas de batata com lombinho de porco* (mashed potato flavored with pork chine), *migas no pingo de entrecosto* (entrecôte), pork cooked in an *alguidar* (a clay pot), and *ensopado de borrego* (lamb stew).

Ponto Final (60)
172, cais do Ginjal, Cacilhas, Almada, 2800 ☎ 276 07 43

🚤 River taxi that leaves from Praça do Comercio ●●● 🕐 daily noon–2am 🍸

To get to Pronto Final, cross the Tagus in one of the river taxis that take about ten minutes from Cais das Colunas (close to Praça do Comércio ➡ 86) to Cais de Ginjal. Whatever time of year you visit, the views over the river, Lisbon, and the bridge ➡ 112 are spectacular. The pig's feet *à la coentrada* (in coriander), and the *xara* are just two of the many specialties. Very sweet cakes. Friendly service. ★ Nearby, on the same quay, a small simple family restaurant, Retiro dos Pescadres, will also delight you with its grilled fish dishes at reasonable prices.

Not forgetting

■ **O Galito (61)** 16-A, rua da Fonte, 1600 ☎ 716 64 75 ●●● 🕐 Mon.–Sat. noon–3pm, 7–10pm; closed public holidays *This tiny restaurant seats 16 maximum and is a real family affair: the mother does the cooking, the father serves at the bar, and the son waits on tables. Come and sample their pure unadulterated dishes from Alentejo, full of style and flavor. The menu includes ensopado de borrego (lamb stew), sopa de cação (shark), pezinhos de porco de coentrada migas (pig's feet in coriander with bread). Special menu during the hunting season. Warm, friendly atmosphere.*

O Galito, further up the Tagus, after visiting Madre de Deus ➡ 96

At the Retiro dos Pescadores (right), on the banks of Ginjal, you can order a meal which is tasty, cheap and filling.

Times

Night life starts late in Lisbon: bars ➡ 64 only begin to fill up after 11pm and nightclubs open around 1am. Locals tend to start their evening out at the movies ➡ 74 or theater ➡ 76 where shows usually begin at 9.30pm.

After dark

Tickets

Tickets for the latest concerts, plays etc., can be bought from the ABEP kiosk on the Praça dos Restauradores or from the box office at the venue itself.

Portuguese coffee

In Portugal, the coffee is as varied as it is delicious:

Café carioca: very weak
Garoto: served with a little milk in a cup
Galão: a large white coffee served in a glass
Bica com cheirinho: served with brandy

Lisbon, the cultural capital of Europe

Ever since Lisbon was voted the cultural capital of Europe in 1994, the artistic climate has gone from strength to strength. A wide variety of shows and performances are on offer each day in one of the city's many quality venues.

Nights out

THE INSIDER'S FAVORITES

What's on...
Agenda Cultural
This monthly magazine is published by the city council and gives details of all cultural events taking place in Lisbon and the surrounding areas. It is available from the Tourist Office, the kiosk at 3 Rua de São Pedro de Alcântara, opposite the São Roque church, or from any public buildings (the town hall, libraries…).

Newspapers
You will also find a good program of cultural and artistic events in the *Expresso*, the *Público* and the *Independente*, published daily.

INDEX BY AREA

Lisbon is one of the last truly Mediterranean cities where an evening stroll and a stop in a bar are well-established customs. True Lisboan culture is found on the street and the most popular meeting places are concentrated in several distinct areas: Bairro Alto, 24 de Julho, Cais do Sodré, and Docas each have their own distinctive characters.

After dark

A Brasileira (1)

120–122, rua Garrett, 1200
☎ 346 95 41
Ⓜ Chiado
🚌 100, 58, tram 28 ⏰ 8–2am

The bronze statue of Fernando Pessoa seated at a table is the symbol of this old café in the Chiado. It has retained its turn-of-the-century decor and attracts a clientele of artists and intellectuals, both young and old.

Captain Kirk (2)

121, rua do Norte, 1200
☎ 343 02 79
🚌 100, 58, tram 28 ⏰ 10.30pm–4am

This new trendy disco with its simple decor is already too small for the crowds of young people who line up to get in. Artistes and musicians visiting Lisbon come to hear bands playing jungle and drum'n'bass.

Pavilhão Chinês (3)

89–91, rua Dom Pedro V, 1200
☎ 342 47 29
🚌 58, 100 ⏰ Mon.–Sat. 6pm–2am; Sun. 9pm–2am

The amazing decor consists of lead figures, china dolls, and Chinese statues on the walls, in cupboards, and hanging down from the ceiling. Don't be deceived by the small tea-tables – the

Pavilhão serves a wide range of cocktails.

British Bar (4)

52–54, rua Bernardino Costa, 1200 ☎ 342 23 67
Ⓜ Cais do Sodré
🚌 numerous, tram 15, 18, 25 ⏰ Sun.–Thurs. 7.30am–midnight; Fri.–Sat. 7.30–2am

At the British Bar; the pace is both relaxed and leisurely. There are 42 different kinds of beer, most of them Belgian. Try the house ginger beer and the house liqueur, digestivo.

Procópio (5)

21-A, alto de S. Francisco, Jardim das Amoreiras, 1250

☎ 385 28 51
Ⓜ Rotunda
⏰ Mon.– Fri. 6pm–3am; Sat. 9pm–3am

An elegant and formal bar. The cocktails are a treat and the prego á casa (steak with a fried egg) is an ideal way to satisfy late-night hunger pangs. The service is impeccable.

Sétimo Céu (6)

54, travessa da Espera, 1200
☎ 346 64 71
🚌 100, 58, tram 28 ⏰ 10pm–2am

A friendly bar popular with artists and intellectuals. The house specialty is Caipirinha, a South American drink made from

Cachaca, lime, and crushed ice — delicious but deceptively strong.

Di Vino (7)

160, rua da Atalaia, 1200
☎ 346 59 88
▣ 100, 58, tram 28 ◲ 7pm–2am

This informal wine bar lists 50 labels, with a bias toward wines from the Alentejo. Try fried chorizo, gizzards, and pork with peppers from the menu of *petiscos* (small snack dishes). There is also a wide selection of fine Alentejo cheeses.

Comodoro (8)

20–23, praça D. João da Câmara, 1200
☎ 346 49 96

Ⓜ Restauradores
◲ Mon.–Sat. 12.30–3pm; 6pm–2.30am

The popular and centrally located Comodoro is a combined bar, nightclub, and restaurant. Wide-ranging clientele.

Bar Irlandês (9)

32–38, rua Cais do Sodré, 1200
☎ 343 10 64
Ⓜ Cais do Sodré
▣ numerous, trams 15, 18, 25
◲ Sun.–Thur. 11.30am–2am; Fri.–Sat. 11.30–4am

This large pub, decorated with souvenirs from the Emerald Isle, stocks the full range of Irish drinks. Its long,

wooden bar is often crowded with uniformed *marinheiros* from the nearby docks.

Crido (10)

53, rua da Glória, 1250 ☎ 342 74 34 Ⓜ Restauradores
◲ Mon.–Sat. 5pm–2am

A trendy techno-style bar which is frequented by a mixed clientele aged 20–60. Its central location makes it an ideal spot to meet and catch up with friends over a coffee or whiskey.

Nova (11)

261, rua da Rosa, 1200 ☎ 346 28 34 ▣ 58, 100
◲ 10pm–2am

Popular with artists and

musicians, the Nova is one of the oldest bars in the Bairro Alto. The decor changes every six months. You can sit in the garden or in the courtyard at the back. Ambient music and DJ.

Web Café (12)

126, rua do Diário de Notícias, 1200
☎ 342 11 81
▣ 100, 58, tram 28 ◲ daily 2pm–2am
@ web1@mail. esolerica.pt

This warm and friendly café is a new arrival to the Bairro Alto. ★ For Esc. 700 an hour, customers can drink coffee or something stronger, surf the Internet, or send electronic mail.

Whether in modern premises or in traditional surroundings, little family-run *tascas* or taverns, are popular eating places. Locals drop in for a drink or a bite to eat at the end of the afternoon before going home or before going out to the bars ➡ 64 discos ➡ 72. Sit at the counter or at a table and sip a glass of wine or a coffee and nibble on some snacks.

After dark

Targus (13)
40-B, rua Diário de Notícias, 1200 ☎ 347 64 03

Ⓜ *Chiado* 🔲 *58, 100* 🕐 *Mon.–Sat. 11am–8pm, 10pm–3am; open daily in summer 11am–8pm, 10pm–3am* ▣ *except Amex*

The large glass front of this café is perhaps a little unexpected given its location in the old quarter of the Bairro. The interior is minimalist and tasteful, and the atmosphere is both warm and friendly. The owner Herâni, a well-known figure in the Bairro Alto, has built up a faithful clientele of journalists and media people. This is definitely the place to come for the latest news.

Estádio (14)
11, rua São Pedro de Alcântara, 1250 ☎ 342 27 56

Ⓜ *Chiado* 🔲 *58, 100* 🕐 *open daily noon–2am: closed sometime in Aug. or Sep.* ▣ 🍴

This cheap, friendly, bustling old café is frequented by the old as well as the young and broke. It was once the haunt of poets and prostitutes, but it now attracts pioneering young intellectuals. At closing time the owner, Manuel, has to encourage his customers, who are always a little reluctant, to leave.

O Pirata (15)
15, praça dos Restauradores, 1250 ☎ 342 78 69

Ⓜ *Restauradores* 🔲 *1, 36, 44, 45* 🕐 *Mon.–Sat. 7am–midnight* ▣ 🍴
🕐 *Specialty:* leite creme

Even if you're just passing through Lisbon or are on a tight schedule, it's worth making time to sample the Pirata's two special drinks: *Pirata* and *Perna do pav*, both of which are registered trademarks. For two generations now the ingredients of these specialties have remained a closely guarded secret. The recipe lies in a sealed envelope in the bottom of a safe and the drinks are made in a special room so that you can't see the ingredients being mixed.

Ginjinha Sem Rival-Eduardino (16)
7, rua das Portas de Santo Antão, 1250

Ⓜ *Restauradores* 🕐 *variable*

Like many other bars in Lisbon, this is a tiny spot that is crammed with bottles and barely able to accommodate half a dozen customers at the bar. The main draw is its delicious specialty, Eduardino liqueur. The excellent *Especial ginjinha* (cherries in brandy) is also recommended. However, beware! These concoctions are deceptively strong!

Not forgetting

■ **Geronte (17)** 33, rua São Pedro de Alcântara, 1250 ☎ 346 80 95
🕐 *daily 9pm–2am The Geronte is crammed with old books, and paintings by contemporary artists hang from floor to ceiling. This is an ideal spot to begin the evening.*

Listening to live music is another popular evening activity in Lisbon. The number of places where you can listen to music played professionally has multiplied over the last few years. These night spots are not really bars and yet not really concert halls either. Jazz, salsa, and tango feature predominantly, while rock seems to be on the wane.

After dark

Hot Clube de Portugal (18)
39, praça da Alegria, 1200 ☎ 346 73 69 ➡ 362 17 41

Ⓜ *Avenida* 🚇 *numerous* 🕐 *Tue.–Sat. 10pm–2am* 🎵 🎵 ***Bands*** *Thur., Fri., Sat.* ***Jam sessions*** *Wed., Thur.* 🍴 🍸

This tiny basement jazz club was founded in 1951 and hosts visiting and local bands. Before the Speakeasy opened, this was the only club in Lisbon where you could go to listen to jazz. In its heyday it used to be completely jam-packed and today remains the best place to hear improvised jazz sessions. If you want a break from the crowds and the smoky atmosphere you can take your drink into courtyard at the back.

Ritz Club (19)
57, rua da Glória, 1250 ☎ 342 51 40 ➡ 315 20 90

Ⓜ *Restauradores, Avenida* 🚇 *numerous* 🕐 *Tue.–Sat. 10pm–4.30am; Sun. 5–9pm* 🎵 🎵 ***Rock and Portuguese popular music*** *Tue., Wed, Thur.* ***Cape Verdean bands*** *Fri., Sat.* 🍴 🍸

The Ritz Club is one of the city's best known and oldest night spots. It used to be a popular theater (the red curtain still remains) and was even a striptease club in the 1930s and 40s. Although the management has changed the old party atmosphere is still very much alive. It hosts alternative rock bands and on the weekends you can dance to Cape Verdean bands.

Paradise Garage (20)
38–48, rua João de Oliveira Minguêns, 1350 ☎ 395 59 77 ➡ 395 71 59

⬛ *Alcântara-Terra* 🚇 *numerous* 🕐 *Thur.–Sat. 12–4am* ⬛ 🎵 ***Various*** 🍸

A chic, modern live-music spot which is situated above the Paradise Café. It is primarily a nightclub which is hosted by well-known DJs and is often the scene of wild partying. ★ There is a comfortable mezzanine floor where you can chill out.

Blues Café (21)
Edifício 226, rua da Cintura do Porto, 1300 ☎ 395 70 85 ➡ 395 71 06

🚌 *14, 28, 32, 43, tram 15, 18* 🕐 *Mon.–Sat. 8pm–4am* ⬛ 🎵 ***Blues and jazz*** *Wed.* 🍴 🍸 🔆 *from 2am onward*

With its traditional Louisiana-style decor, the Blues Café is the most luxurious and elegant nightspot on the Tagus waterfront. It gets its name from the blues and jazz evenings that are held here every Wednesday evening. As well as being a bar-restaurant and disco, it also hosts conferences, fashion shows, and a variety of different business and cultural events.

Not forgetting

■ **Speakeasy (22)** Armazém 115, cais das Oficinas, Rocha Conde d'Óbidos, 1350 ☎ 395 73 08 🕐 *Mon.–Sat. noon–3pm, 6pm–4am* *Bar-restaurant with jazz and blues from 11pm onward.*

Fado vitória, fado corrido, and *fado menor* are all varieties of a musical tradition which goes back to the last century. Full of nostalgia and yearning, *fado* celebrates the past, the sea, love and Lisbon itself. It has managed to adapt and change with the times, and the big names make way for younger singers. *Fado* places are often hidden in unexpected spots.

After dark

Senhor Vinho (23)
18, rua do Meio à Lapa, 1200 ☎ 397 26 81 ➡ 395 20 72

Ⓜ *Avenida* 🚌 *27, tram 28* 🕐 *Mon.–Sat. 10pm–2.30am* ●●● *Esc. 6000–6500 including meal* 🔲 🎵 *open daily* 🍴 🍸

A *fado* restaurant where you can hear one of the most prestigious *fadistas* (*fado* singers): the great Maria da Fe, a well-known local singer. The decor is traditional, the objects that hang on the walls all have a story behind them. Lisbon high society comes here to enjoy fine cuisine and to listen to singers of what is known as *fado castico* – Maria Dilar, Camane, Jorge Fernando, Carlos Madedo, Paulo Saraiva, Maria Amelia, and Audina Duarte. An unforgettable place.

Arcadas do Faia (24)
56, rua da Barroca, 1200 ☎ 342 67 42 ➡ 342 19 23

Ⓜ *Chiado* 🚌 *58, 100* 🕐 *Mon.–Sat. 8pm–2.30am* ●●● *Esc. 5000–6000 including meal* 🔲 🎵 *open daily* 🍴 🍸

The group of singers who perform at the Arcadas do Faia are among the most popular in the Bairro Alto. Lenita Gentil, Vasco Rafael, Anita Guerreiro, Alice Pires, and Maria do Rosario perform a repertoire of Lisbon *fados* beneath the arched ceilings. The emotionally powerful music is complemented by fine, traditional cuisine and chic, elegant surroundings.

Adega do Machado (25)
91, rua do Norte, 1200 ☎ 346 00 95 ➡ 346 75 07

Ⓜ *Chiado* 🚌 *58, 100* 🕐 *Tue.–Sun. 8.30pm–3am* ●●● *Esc. 6000 including meal* 🔲 🎵 *open daily* 🍴 🍸

A long-standing, authentic *fado* spot. Some of Portugal's best-known *fado* singers perform here. Ana de Carvalho, Marina Rosa, Maria Jose Valerio, and Fernando de Sousa sing *fados* from Lisbon, while Carlos Pocinho sings the more light-hearted *fado* music of Coïmbra. Folk dancing from the Minho and Ribatejo regions rounds off the evening and often everyone joins in.

Café Luso (26)
10, travessa da Queimada, 1200 ☎ 342 22 81 ➡ 347 83 20

Ⓜ *Chiado* 🚌 *58, 100* 🕐 *Mon.–Sat. 8pm–2am; closed Dec. 24 and 25* ●●● *Esc. 6000 including meal; Esc. 3500 including drink only* 🔲 🎵 *open daily* 🍴 🍸

Café Luso is one of the oldest and most famous *fado* spots. Two of Portugal's greatest *fadistas* have sung here: Amália Rodrigues and Alfredo Marceniero. The building, which dates back to before the earthquake, used to house the coachmen employed at the São Roque palace.

Not forgetting
■ **Parreirinha de Alfama (27)** 1, beco do Espírito Santo, 1100 ☎ 886 82 09 *This touristy fado restaurant is particularly known for its cuisine* ➡ 42.

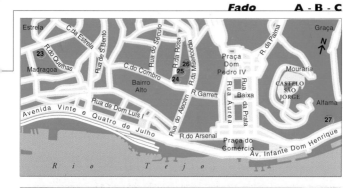

25

The legendary Amália Rodrigues, one of the most celebrated *fado* singers in the world, interprets the words of the great Portuguese poets in song.

For some unknown reason, the major dance spots in Lisbon tend to be concentrated near the Tagus, either on Avenida 24 de Julho or on Cais de Alcântara. Those who prefer more intimate bars have no choice at dawn but to join the crowds. The discos, most of them free, mop up the late-night revelers.

After dark

Alcântara-Mar (28)
11, rua da Cozinha Económica, 1300 ☎ 363 64 32 ➡ 362 29 48

Alcântara-Terra ▣ numerous, tram 15, 18 ◷ Tue., Thur.–Sat. 12–6am
▤ ▼

The Alcântara-Mar is a huge, extravagant nightspot which plays house music and techno. It is quite eccentric, with its framed portraits of austere-looking subjects, its gilded columns, crimson velvet walls, purple curtains, and chandeliers. The club also organizes regular live music events featuring local bands.

Frágil (29)
128, rua da Atalaia, 1200 ☎ 346 95 78

Ⓜ Restauradores, Rossio ▣ numerous ◷ Tue.–Sat. 11.30pm–4am ▣ ▼

This bar-disco has become something of an institution and has transformed the night scene in the area since it opened ten years ago. It is frequented by trendy types of all ages. Don't worry about bumping into people, the heaving crowds are all part of the atmosphere. The decor is regularly redone by local artists. There are a number of rooms, each with a different ambience.

Kremlin (30)
5, escadinhas da Praia, 1200 ☎ 390 87 68 ➡ 395 71 02

Alcântara ▣ 14, 28, 32, 43, tram 15, 18 ◷ Tue.–Sat. midnight–8am ▤ ▼

The first disco in Lisbon to concentrate solely on dance music. This is where you'll find the DJ Vibe, from the Underground Sound of Lisbon, the most international of all the Portuguese groups. Recently this house/techno club was expanded to double its size.

Salsa Latina (31)
Gare Marítima de Alcântara, 1350 ☎ 395 05 55 ➡ 395 05 41

Alcântara ▣ 14, 28, 32, 43, tram 15, 18 ◷ Mon.–Sat. 8pm–6am ▤
♫ bands Tue.–Sat. ▼ ▥ meal ●●● Esc.4000–5000

The Salsa Latina, located on the Tagus waterfront, is one of the hottest dance spots of the moment. There is a distinct Caribbean ambience, with the resident band playing predominantly salsa music. It's not difficult to have fun in this lively and friendly club. ★ Bring suitable shoes.

Not forgetting

■ **Kapital (32)** 68, avenida 24 de Julho, 1300 ☎ 346 95 78 ◷ daily 11pm–5am *If it's rock rather than house music that gets your feet tapping then this is the place to come. Unusual decor, splendid terrace, business types.*
■ **Trumps (33)** 104-B, rua da Imprensa Nacional, 1250 ☎ 397 10 59 ◷ daily 11pm–4am *Gay disco, house music.*
■ **King's & Queen's (34)** rua da Cintura do Porto, pavilhão H, 1300 ☎ 397 76 99 ◷ Mon.–Sat. 10pm–4am *Gay pride disco. Eccentric dancers and drag queens.*

In Lisbon not many of the big old movie theaters survived the movie crisis of the 1980s; many have shut or been torn down. These days, you are more likely to find the most interesting movies at the new movie houses. Tickets cost around Esc. 700.

After dark

Cinemateca Portuguesa (35)
39, rua Barata Salgueiro, 1250 ☎ 354 62 79 ➡ 352 31 80

Ⓜ Rotunda 🎬 *numerous* 🕐 **Screenings** *Mon.–Fri. 6.30pm, 9.30pm; Sat. 3.30pm, 6.30pm, 9.30pm. Closed Aug.* ● *Esc. 350* 🔲 🔳

At a time when the popularity of the movie theater was at an all-time low in Portugal, the Cinemateca, a sanctuary for cinephiles, was the only place where young directors could hope to show their work. Today it has moved away from showcasing new talent and concentrates instead on showing classics and neglected movies from the past. The Cinemateca's charismatic manager, João Bénard da Costa, starred in movies by Manoel de Oliveira and João César Monteiro, Portugal's best-known and most popular directors.

São Jorge (36)
175, avenida da Liberdade, 1298 ☎ 357 91 44 ➡ 357 93 44

Ⓜ Avenida 🎬 *numerous* 🕐 **screen 1** *3.30pm, 6.30pm, 9.30pm* **screen 2** *2pm, 4.30pm, 7pm, 9.40pm* **screen 3** *2.15pm, 4.45pm, 7.15pm, 9.45pm* ● *Esc. 750, Mon. Esc. 550* 🔲 🔳

One of Lisbon's last great movie theaters, although the original theater is now divided up into three smaller screens. It was built in 1950 when movie-going was at its height in Lisbon. In screen 1, which has seats for 850, something of the old atmosphere still lingers. There is still an interval, although these days the movie is more than likely to be a Hollywood blockbuster.

King Triplex (37)
52, avenida Frei Miguel Contreiras, 1700 ☎ 848 08 08 ➡ 848 08 08

Ⓜ Roma 🎬 *7, 27, 33, 35, 67* 🕐 *variable* ● *Esc. 750, Mon. Esc. 500* 🔲 🔳 🔳

This movie theater, located beneath the Maria Matos theater and run by the producer and director, Paulo Branco, champions alternative cinema. His three screens are entirely devoted to quality movies – independent American releases and European productions (which make up 80 per cent of the screenings). Portuguese movies are also shown here. There is also a bar and bookstore on site.

Monumental (38)
71, avenida Praia da Vitória, 1050 ☎ 353 18 59 ➡ 353 45 32

Ⓜ Saldanha 🎬 *numerous* 🕐 *variable* ● *Esc.750, Mon. Esc. 500* 🔲 🔳

One of the largest movie theaters in Lisbon. Since opening three more screens, its programing has been a compromise between good quality movies and the more popular fare.

Not forgetting

■ **Mundial (39)** 12-A, rua Martins Ferrão, 1050 ☎ 353 87 43 *A popular 1930s-style theater.*

■ **Nimas (40)** 42-B, avenida 5 de Outubro, 1050 ☎ 357 43 62 *Opened in the 1970s, screens independent and avant-garde movies.*

Live theater and performances have expanded in Portugal over the last ten years to include classical and modern pieces as well as *teatro de revista* which brings politics and current affairs to the stage. A number of free concerts is held in churches (Sé et São Roque, Basilica de Estrela, Basilica da Nossa Senhora dos Mártires, and Convento do Carmo).

After dark

Teatro Nacional D. Maria II (41)
Praça Dom Pedro IV, 1100 ☎ 347 22 46 ➡ 343 15 35

ⓜ *Restauradores, Rossio* 🚌 *numerous* 🕐 *Garrett Theater Tue., Sat. 9.30pm; Sun. 4pm Studio Tue., Sat. 9.45pm; Sun. 4.30pm. Closed Aug.* ● *Esc. 1500–3500 Ticket office Tue.–Sun. 2–9.30pm* 🖵 🛈

Set up by the playwright Almeida Garrett, the author of *Frei Luís de Sousa*, this great theater was built in 1846 to house the National Theater Company, still going strong today. The Garrett Theater and the Studio put on classics and contemporary plays respectively. The director Carlos Avilez is head of the theater. ★ There is also a specialist bookstore.

Teatro do Bairro Alto (42)
1-A, rua Tenente Raúl Cascais, 1250 ☎ 396 15 15 ➡ 395 45 08

ⓜ *Marquês de Pombal, Rotunda* 🚌 *58, 100* 🕐 *Performances 9.30pm* ● *Esc. 2000 Ticket office Tue.–Fri. 2.30–10pm; Sat.–Sun. 1.30–4.30pm* 🖵 🛈

Since 1995, this theater has been home to the Teatro Da Cornucópia company, directed by one of its founders, the actor and director, Luís Miguel Cintra. Since its creation in 1973, this troupe has seen 175 actors come and go and is today the best example of independent Portuguese theater.

Coliseu dos Recreios (43)
96, rua das Portas de Santa Antão, 1150 ☎ 343 16 77 ➡ 342 04 34

ⓜ *Restauradores* 🚌 *1, 19, 21, 80* 🕐 *Performances daily 9.30pm* ● *Esc. 3000 Ticket office open daily 1–7pm. Closed in Aug.* 🖵 🛈

The largest hall in Lisbon now has even better facilities and acoustics since the work undertaken in 1994, the year that Lisbon was voted Cultural Capital of Europe. Its circular construction bears some resemblance to London's Royal Albert Hall. It was originally designed as a circus ring, and circus shows still take place here in December. All kinds of events are hosted, but music tends to dominate. Madredeus, José Afonso, and Amália Rodrigues have all performed here.

Teatro Municipal de S. Luís (44)
40, rua Antónia Maria Cardoso, 1200 ☎ 342 71 72 ➡ 347 68 58

ⓜ *Chiado* 🚌 *58, 100, tram 28* 🕐 *Performances daily 9.30pm* ● *Esc. 2500–3000 Ticket office Tue.–Sun. 2–8pm; days when there are performances 2–10pm* 🖵 🛈

This is both a light comedy theater and home to an independent theater company, the Companhia Teatral do Chiado, formed by one of Portugal's greatest actors, Mario Viegas.

Not forgetting

■ **Chapitô (45)** 1, Costa do Castelo, 1100 ☎ 887 82 25 *The Chapito theater-circus company has taken up residence near the São Jorge castle.*
■ **Teatro Nacional de São Carlos (46)** 9, rua Serpa Pinto, 1200 ☎ 346 59 14 *This old theater has become Lisbon's opera house.*

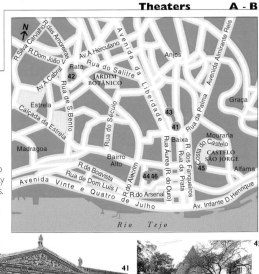

The imposing Teatro do Rossio is open every day for performances. There is also a café and a book store.

Lisbon's cultural institutions, both national and international, have flourished since 1974 when Portugal opened itself to the outside world. The famous Fundação Calouste Gulbenkian has also had a positive effect. These institutions serve as educational centers, meeting places, and venues for concerts, theater, dance, ballet, and recitals.

After dark

Fundação Calouste Gulbenkian (47)
45-A, avenida de Berna, 1067 ☎ 793 51 31 ➡ 793 51 39

M *São Sebastião, Espanha* 🚌 *16, 26, 31, 41, 46* 🕐 *Performances 7pm, 9pm* ● *Esc. 2000–5000 Foundation 9am–1pm, 2.30–5.30pm Museum ➡ 100*

This is Portugal's largest cultural institution and organizes extensive programs of classical and contemporary music and dance, modern art exhibitions, and summertime open-air jazz in summer are just some of the cultural activities that are organized by the country's largest cultural institution. The foundation, which is committed to fostering public interest in music, dance, and song, has formed its own groups of performers and musicians who attain the highest standards. The foundation also houses a movie theater, a theater, the country's most important collection of 20th-century Portuguese art, and the Calouste Gulbenkian collection ➡ 98.

Culturgest (48)
Portaria da rua do Arco do Cego, 1000 ☎ 790 51 55 ➡ 848 39 03

M *Campo Pequeno* 🚌 *1, 36, 83* 🕐 *Performances 9pm, matinee 5pm Ticket office open daily 1–7pm* ● *Esc. 1000–4000 Exhibition room 1 10am–6pm; room 2 11am–8pm*

The Culturgest, with its two auditoriums and exhibition spaces, is Lisbon's most recent cultural foundation. There are modern art exhibitions and dance, music, theater and film festivals with accompanying lecture series. These events, particularly the lectures, are popular and well attended so booking is highly recommended.

Centro Cultural de Belém (49)
Praça do Império ☎ 361 24 00 ➡ 361 25 00

Belém 🚌 *27, 28, 29, 43, 49, 51, tram 15* 🕐 *Performances 11am, 9.30pm* ● *Esc. 1000–4000 Ticket office open daily 1–7.30pm Exhibits ➡ 106*

The program of events at the Centro Cultural de Belém is more varied than at the Culturgest and slightly more popular than at the Fundáço Calouste Gulbenkian. The imposing building (unfinished) overlooks the Tagus. ★ As well as providing space for a wide variety of different cultural events and exhibitions, the center also hosts late-afternoon concerts in the Jardim das Oliveiras.

Not forgetting
■ **Casa Fernando Pessoa (50)** 16, rua Coelho da Rocha, 1250 ☎ 396 81 99 *Located in the charming area of Campo Ourique, the poet's house hosts permanent and temporary exhibits, recitals, and poetry readings. It also publishes a review.*
■ **Instituto Cervantes (51)** 43, rua de Santa Marta, 1150 ☎ 352 31 21 *Spanish lessons, film festivals, and concerts.*
■ **Institut franco-português (52)** 91, avenida Luís Bivar, 1150 ☎ 311 14 00 *Busy program of theater, cinema, and music.*
■ **Instituto Italiano (53)** 146, rua do Salitre, 1250 ☎ 388 41 72 *Language classes and cultural events held in a 17th-century building.*

Lisbon by bus
A number of travel agencies
organize tours of the city.
Carris guided tours ➡ 12
☎ 363 20 44

 **What to see**

**Lisbon by
boat**
Compagnie
Transtejo ➡ 12
Estação Fluvial,
Terreiro do
Paço, 1200
☎ 887 50 58

**Lisbon by
tram**
**Numbers 15
and 17**: to travel
along the Tagus
from Baixa to
Belém
Number 24:
to get from Chiado
to Amoreiras
Number 28:
for a look at the
oldest districts;
Graça, Alfama, Baixa,
Chiado and Estrela

Subway stations
Rotunda: portrait of the Marquês de Pombal
Campo Pequeno: life-size sculptures of horses and bulls
Entre Campos: tribute to Portuguese literature (the library is situated
just above) **Sete Rios**: drawings of flora and fauna (the Jardim Zoológico
is situated just above) **Picoas**: tribute to the Paris subway

Sights

THE INSIDER'S FAVORITES

The seventh hill

Like Rome, Lisbon is a city built on seven hills, but for centuries there have been disagreements about this number. However, since 1994 Lisbon has decided to publicize its seventh hill. A tram tour will take you from hill to hill and will reveal the architectural riches of the city.

Tram Tours dep. Praça do Comércio
☎ 363 93 43 from Mar. 1 to Oct. 19
Mon.–Sun. 11.30am, 1.30pm,
2.30pm, 3.30pm, 4.30pm
● Esc. 2800; children Esc. 1500

INDEX BY TYPE

"For the traveler who comes in from the sea, Lisbon, even from afar, rises like a fair vision in a dream, clear-cut against a bright blue sky which the sun gladdens with its gold. And the domes, the monuments, the old castles jut up above the mass of houses, like far-off heralds of this delightful seat, of this blessed region." *Fernando Pessoa*

➡ What to see

For centuries Lisbon turned its attention to the open sea and its colonies and was then ruled for 40 years by a dictatorship. Both of these facts led it to become a city cut off from the rest of Europe. Tucked away on its seven hills ➡ 80 and in its narrow streets are palaces, gardens and old buildings where craftsmen, shoe-shine boys and all variety of store keepers still ply their trade. A mixture of both the rich and working-class, the **white city** with its limestone façades is reflected in the golden waters of the Tagus estuary (*Rio Tejo*), nicknamed the **sea of straw** (*mar de palha*). Strategically positioned as a port town on the route between the Mediterranean and the Atlantic Ocean, Lisbon was the envy of all and was occupied over the centuries by the Romans, the Alani and the Visigoths. Under the Moors (716–1147) it was named Lissabona (the wonderful harbor) and underwent its first real period of expansion. In the 15th century, Portugal set off to conquer the world. This was **the Age of Discoveries**, when expeditions were sent to the Indies, Brazil and Africa. With slaves, cloth, spices and precious metals passing through its port, Lisbon was at its peak. During these periods at sea, the sailors would long to be home, but on their return, would be filled with yearnings for distant lands. This melancholy, known as **saudade**, finds its most poignant expression in the **fado** ➡ 70. This tradition was born in the cabarets of Mouraria in the 14th century and still echoes around the old districts of Alfama, Mouraria and Graça, the sole remaining areas of medieval Lisbon after the **earthquake of 1755**. The earthquake claimed more than 40,000 lives and destroyed the center of the city. Rebuilding was placed in the hands of the **Marquês de Pombal** who dreamed of a Lisbon based on a geometric plan where wide thoroughfares would intersect each other at right angles. The "low quarter" was razed to

the ground and Baixa rebuilt according to his plans. To protect the buildings from fire, they were covered with panels of **azulejos** (from the words *azul*, blue and *zulej*, smooth), glazed ceramic tiles invented by the Moors and brought to Portugal by the Spanish in the 16th century. The city is adorned with blue and white frescos depicting a Lisbon that has vanished. While the practice of paving also dates back to the 16th century, the earthquake brought a renewed interest in this art form. Paved with small pieces of limestone and basalt, the ground in places is transformed into elaborate colorful mosaics. The best way to get around the city is on foot or by tram, with its many hills and valleys making it constantly necessary to climb steps or take elevators or funiculars. From the top of one of the many viewing platforms, you will always be able to make out the Tagus and the outline of the bridge connecting the city to the opposite bank. Built under **Salazar** (1889–1970), it was renamed the **Ponte 25 de Abril** ➡ 112 to commemorate the Captain's Revolution that overturned the dictatorship on April 25, 1974, without a single shot being fired. The arrival of thousands of refugees following the independence of Portugal's African colonies has made Lisbon a highly cosmopolitan city. The postmodern towers rising in the north of the city contrast sharply with the old districts around the **Castelo São Jorge** ➡ 90 which have something of a village air about them. Each summer, pagan rituals and religious ceremonies combine in festivals to commemorate popular saints. On June 13, the people of Lisbon celebrate the life of **Saint Anthony of Padua**. After the religious procession of the afternoon, tables and *braseros* are set up in the streets to serve grilled sardines and as much wine as you can drink. In 1998 the 21st century will be celebrated in Lisbon when it plays host to **Expo '98** ➡ 114.

This square is the start of Avenida da Liberdade, the city's main avenue, paved with marble and basalt. West of the square lies the pedestrianized Rua das Portas de Santo Antão lined with museums and old buildings. In the east São Pedro hill marks the border with Bairro Alto. ■ Where to

What to see

Praça dos Restauradores (1)

Ⓜ *Restauradores, Rossio*

The obelisk standing in the middle of Praça dos Restauradores was erected in 1886 to commemorate the rebellion of 1640 which brought the Duke of Bragança to power and freed Portugal from 60 years of Spanish rule. To the southwest of the square, on the small *largo* Dom João da Câmara, stands the Estação do Rossio, which is tucked away in an attractive neo-Manueline building. The trains going to Sintra ➡ 14 and Leiria all leave from this station. To the west, the Foz Palace, which was built by Francisco Fabri, was originally the residence of the Marquês de Castelo Melhor, then, in 1889, became the family home of the Marquês de Foz, before becoming an important cultural center which attracted Lisbon high society. Its collections have now been dispersed and today it houses the tourist office ➡ 14. ★ Right next to the square, you can catch the Calçada da Glória which will take you up the hillside as far as São Roque.

Igreja / Museu de São Roque (2)
Largo Trindade Coelho ☎ 323 50 60 ➡ 323 50 60

Ⓜ *Restauradores, Chiado* 🕐 *Tue.–Sun. 10am–5pm; closed public holidays* ● *Esc. 150; students and under-18s free* 🔲 🔳 *reservation required* 🔠

This church was built between 1566 and 1575 by Filippo Terzi (who was also responsible for building the monastery of São Vicente de Fora ➡ 94). Do not be put off by its rather plain façade, for once inside, the ornate decoration is quite astonishing. The Italianate painting on the wooden ceiling of the nave is the work of Francisco Venegas and depicts the victory of the Holy Cross (1584–90). Each of the chapels is a masterpiece of Italian baroque art, where gilded, carved wooden altar screens stand alongside *azulejos*. The showpiece, however, is the late-baroque São Baptista chapel where lapis lazuli columns, marble statues, precious stones, and gilded bronze statues rise above a floor itself covered with richly colored mosaics. Entirely constructed in Rome at the request of João V, it was then dismantled, transported by boat to Lisbon, and rebuilt in 1747. Next door to the church, a small museum houses a few of the treasures of São Baptista including ceremonial robes, gold and silver objects by Italian artists that were used during religious services, and some works of art by 16th-century Portuguese painters.

Miradouro de São Pedro de Alcântara (3)
Rua São Pedro de Alcântara

To enjoy a view over the whole of Lisbon, climb one of the seven hills surrounding the city. In just a few minutes, the Calçada da Glória takes you from Praça dos Restauradores to the upper part of town (Bairro Alto). ★ A beautiful park on the edges of a small lake has been laid out on São Pedro hill from where there are splendid views over Rossio, Restauradores, Avenida da Liberdade, the Castelo São Jorge ➡ 90, Sé Cathedral ➡ 92, and the districts of Graça, Mouraria and Alfama. There is also a map made of *azulejos* which, although out of date, will still help you to identify the sites.

This painting of the *Nativity and Adoration*, dating from 1520, is one of many works of art you can see in the Museu de São Roque.

In the area

In the Middle Ages, the streets in Baixa were named according to the crafts practised there: Rua da Prata (silver), Rua do Ouro (gold), and Rua Augusta (main). Today, these crafts have gone but Baixa remains the main shopping center. ■ Where to stay ➡ 19 ➡ 20 ■ Where to eat ➡ 34

What to see

Praça Dom Pedro IV / Praça do Rossio (4)

Ⓜ *Rossio, Restauradores*

Dating from the 13th century, this square is still sometimes referred to by its medieval name, Praça do Rossio. Before the earthquake and fires of 1755, it was surrounded by some of the most impressive buildings in the city. In the center stand two baroque fountains (carved in France), and a monument that was erected in 1870 to Dom Pedro IV, the first king of Brazil. On the north side of the square, on the site of the Palácio de Inquisição (where public executions were carried out during the Inquisition), stands the Teatro Nacional Dona Maria II ➡ 76, one of the neoclassical buildings designed by Pombal's architects after the earthquake. On top of its façade, complete with peristyle and pediment, stands a statue of Gil Vicente, the father of Portuguese theater. From Praça Dom Pedro IV, there is a pleasant walk along any of the three parallel roads which cross the district of Baixa to Praça do Comércio. Rua do Ouro (also called Rua Áurea), Rua da Prata, and Rua Augusta all lead to the impressive, baroque triumphal arch (19th-century) on Praça do Comércio. In the basement of the Banco de Credito Portugues, at the angle formed by the Rua da Prata and the Rua dos Correiros, are the remains of some Roman baths.

Elevador de Santa Justa / Ouro-Carmo (5)
Rua do Ouro / Rua de Santa Justa

Ⓜ *Restauradores, Rossio* Ⓩ *daily 7am–midnight* ● *Esc. 150* 🔁 🔀

Up a few steps at the far end of Rua do Ouro is the entrance to the Santa Justa elevator, originally called Ouro-Carmo since it covers the 90 ft that separate Santa Justa (Baixa) and Praça do Carmo (Chiado). ★ This neo-Gothic construction, the work of the French-born Portuguese engineer Raoul Mesnier du Ponsard who was heavily influenced by Gustave Eiffel, was extremely daring for its time (1898), and was originally powered by steam.

Eraça do Comércio / Terreiro do Paço (6)

This is without doubt the most beautiful square in the city. Renamed Praça do Comércio during the time of Pombal, it is sometimes referred to by its original name, Terreiro do Paço. In the past, it served as the esplanade of the Royal Palace of Ribeira (one of the largest libraries in Europe) which, like many other buildings, was destroyed by the earthquake of 1755. The square, designed by Carlos Mardel and Eugénio dos Santos, is on a par with the vast squares that were built in Europe during the 17th and 18th centuries. Praça do Comércio was intended to symbolize new Lisbon, organized around a geometric plan. The classical buildings and arcades around the edges of the square form a severe, noble and elegant ensemble that today houses the Stock Exchange and various different government ministries. In the center stands a bronze statue of King José I on horseback by the sculptor Machado de Castro (1775). ★ From the Cais das Colunas, to the south of the square, you have a plunging view over the Tagus and its opposite bank where the imposing outlines of the Cristo Rei ➡ 112 and the Ponte 25 de Abril ➡ 112 stand out.

➥ 35 ➥ 36➥ 38 ■ After dark
➥ 76 ■ What to see ➥ 88 ➥
92 ■ Where to shop ➥ 130
➥ 132 ➥ 134 ➥ 142

The district of Chiado was once the meeting place of men of letters and home to some of Lisbon's most sophisticated stores. This area of art galleries and bookstores is dotted with statues of the poets and writers that made it famous. ■ Where to stay ➡ 20 ■ Where to eat ➡ 38

What to see

Igreja / Museu do Carmo (7)
Largo do Carmo, 1200 ☎ ➡ 346 04 73

Ⓜ *Restauradores, then the Santa Justa elevator* ➡ *86* Ⓒ *museum and church Mon.–Sat. 10am–1pm, 2pm–5pm; closed public holidays* ● *Esc. 300* 🎫

The do Carmo monastery and church were built in 1389 under the supervision of Nuno Álvares Pereira. This remnant of medieval Lisbon largely withstood the earthquake of 1755 and only the nave of the imposing Gothic building was destroyed, leaving it open to the sky. This has now been transformed into a garden and decorated with *azulejos*. The building itself has not been touched since the earthquake. The museum contains prehistoric, Roman, and pre-Columbian objects as well as a number of 12th-century tombs.

Igreja Nossa Senhora de Loreto (8)
2, rua da Misericórdia, 1200

🚌 *58, tram 28* Ⓒ *daily 7am–12.30pm, 3–7pm* ● *no admission charge*

Built in 1573 by the architect Marcos de Magalhães, the original church was razed to the ground following the earthquake of 1755. The new church, built in 1785 by José da Costa e Silva, retains the sober and noble proportions of its predecessor, combining mannerist and neoclassical styles. The Italianate decoration has earned it the nickname the Italians' church, but the presence of polychrome *azulejos* constantly remind visitors that they are still in Lisbon.

Le Chiado d'Álvaro Siza Vieira (9)
Rua do Carmo / Rua Nova do Almada / Rua Garrett, 1200

The inhabitants of Lisbon still remember the dreadful fire that swept through parts of the city on the night of August 25, 1988, destroying some of the most beautiful buildings of the Chiado. Following the fire, an international controversy arose over whether to rebuild the area as before or to rebuild in a more contemporary style of architecture. Eventually, Álvaro Siza Vieira proposed a compromise, retaining the proportions and level of decoration of the Pombaline period while integrating features of a more contemporary style.

Not forgetting

■ **Museu do Chiado (10)** 6, rua Serpa Pinto, 1200 ☎ 343 21 48 ➡ 343 21 51 Ⓒ *Tue. 2–6pm; Wed.–Sun. 10am–6pm Portuguese works of art from the 19th and 20th centuries, housed in a former biscuit factory, remodeled by the French architect Jean-Michel Wilmotte.*
■ **Teatro Nacional de São Carlos (11)** 9, rua Serpa Pinto, 1200 ☎ 346 84 08 ➡ 347 17 38 Ⓒ *Mon.–Fri. 1–7pm A neoclassical fronted opera house, built in 1792. Its archways, Doric columns, and terrace recall those of the Saint Charles theater in Naples* ➡ *76.*
■ **Igreja Nossa Senhora da Encarnação (12)** 15, largo do Chiado, 1200 ☎ 342 46 23 Ⓒ *Mon.–Fri. 7am–12.30pm, 3–7pm; Sat., Sun. and public holidays 7am–12.30pm, 4–7pm Built in 1793, this church has a rococo-style pediment decorated with a neoclassical bas-relief. The lavish and exuberant decoration of the interior is surprising.*

The rebuilt Chiado with its
contemporary interiors
and its classically
proportioned façades.

Experience the real charm of Lisbon by losing yourself in the maze
of narrow alleyways that wind around the castle through the districts
of Mouraria and Graça, filled with the distant air of *fados*. Every year
on the evening of June 12, the whole of Lisbon gathers in these old

What to see

Castelo São Jorge (13)
Costa do Castelo, 1170 ☎ 887 17 22

🚊 37 🕐 *daily 9am–11pm* ● *no admission charge* 🏛

The castle has been inhabited by a variety of different occupants, from
the Romans and the Visigoths to the Moors and the first Portuguese
monarchs. Over the centuries it has undergone a number of structural
changes and according to popular myth, secret tunnels and passages were
added during the Middle Ages. Haughty and sturdy, it dominates the city
at its feet. Today it seems to be of limited architectural interest, and this
is because many of its interesting features have been lost over the past
two centuries. From the beautiful gardens containing *jacarandás* and
micocouliers (trees imported from Brazil) there is a wonderful view
overlooking the whole town. Inside its walls lie a pretty little village and
quaint church.

Igreja da Graça (14)
Largo da Graça, 1170 ☎ 887 39 43 ➡ 888 02 15

🚊 *tram 17, 12, 28* 🕐 *daily 9.30am–noon, 3.30–7.30pm* ● *no admission charge*

Started in 1271 and rebuilt many times since, this monument is central to
the district and is a strange mixture of architectural styles: a Manueline
baptistery, a baroque bell tower, a sober classical nave, and a regular
geometrical façade typical of the Pombaline period. The interior is equally
as diverse. The chapels are decorated with baroque gilded woodcarvings,
while in the choir stands an impressive high altar carved to represent
richly embroidered fabric. Magnificent corridors completely covered with
azulejos lead to the sacristy. ★ On your way out, don't miss the Palácio de
Vale de Reis, an impressive building completely covered with *azulejos*. Also
make a slight detour via the Miradouro da Graça to take in the views over
the northern ramparts of the castle

Museu das Artes Decorativas (15)
2, largo das Portas do Sol, 1100
☎ 886 21 83 or 888 19 91 ➡ 887 21 73

🚊 *tram 17, 12, 28* 🕐 *Mon., Wed.–Sun. 10am–5pm* ● *Esc. 800; over-65s
Esc. 400; under-12s free*

Exhibits include everyday Portuguese furniture from the 17th and 18th
centuries, *azulejos* from various palaces and *quintas*, and works of art by
a number of Portuguese and foreign artists.

Not forgetting

■ **Miradouro Santa Luzia (16)** Largo de Santa Luzia, 1200 *Decorated
with azulejos, the viewing platform offers a breathtaking view of the Ponte 25 de
Abril* ➡ *112. Next to it, the Igreja Santa Luzia was built in the 18th century on
the Cerca moura (Moorish walls). Behind a simple façade are a number of tombs
and two panels of azulejos by António Quaresma depicting the conquest of Lisbon
and the Royal Palace before the earthquake. The interior has now fallen into a bad
state of repair and is unfortunately closed to the public.*

working-class districts to
celebrate St Anthony's Day.
■ Where to stay ➡ 18 ■
After dark ➡ 76

In the area

Alfama is one of the most unspoilt districts of Lisbon. In this web of *becos* (dead ends) and alleyways linked by small stairways, you will still find a mixture of cultures, open-air markets, small craft stores and cheap restaurants. ■ Where to stay ➡ 18 ■ Where to eat ➡ 34 ➡ 38

What to see

Sé Patriarcal (17)
Largo da Sé, 1100

▣ tram 28 ◯ Tue.–Sat. 9am–5pm ● **Cloisters** Esc. 100, **Treasures** Esc. 400
▣

According to accounts of the period, the cathedral was built after the conquest of Lisbon (1147) on the site of a mosque. It is the only remaining monument to date from the foundation of the Portuguese nation, although it has been modified, enlarged, and rebuilt many times over the years following the wishes of kings and the esthetic fashions of the day. This simple and imposing structure is built on a cross-shaped plan, typical of Roman churches of the period. The main nave, supported by large simple Roman arches, stands alongside a baroque choir, an ambulatory with lancet windows, and Gothic radiating chapels. The chapel of Bartolomeu Joanes houses the famous terracotta crib by Machado de Castrotandis, while in the choir lies the tomb of Afonso IV. The Roman cloisters, which are decorated with Gothic arches, contain a magnificent Moorish wrought iron gate. The cathedral also has a museum of treasures in which a number of ceremonial robes and a large collection of Portuguese religious objects in silver and goldare displayed.

Igreja de Santo António da Sé (18)
24, largo de Santo António da Sé, 1100

▣ 37, tram 28 ◯ daily 8am–7.30pm ● no admission charge

This church, built on the site of the home of Saint Anthony of Padua, has become a center of popular worship. Each year on June 13, celebrations take place in honor of St Anthony ➡ 82, the miracle worker. Originally erected during the reign of João II, the church was completely rebuilt by the architect Mateus Vicente, opening for services in 1787 and completed in 1812. From the fan staircase leading to the entrance, take a moment to admire the façade and baroque pediment. Inside, the wooden ceilings are decorated to look like marble while the altars are covered with paintings by Pedro Alexandrino de Carvalha who worked on many other churches that were rebuilt after the earthquake. ★ The statue of St Anthony stands in the large choir. Miraculously spared by the earthquake, it is carried each year in the St Anthony's Day procession. The Antoniano Museum, opened in 1962 in a small room next to the church, brings together collections of drawings and paintings donated to the city and various objects connected with popular worship.

Not forgetting

■ **Igreja da Conceição Velha (19)** Rua da Alfândega, 1100
◯ daily 8am–1pm; 3.30–7pm *This church, the south façade of which survived the earthquake, contains Manueline sculptures and a mannerist chapel.*
■ **Igreja de Santa Maria Madalena (20)** Largo da Madalena, 1100
◯ Mon.–Fri. 8am–12.30pm, 4–7pm; Sat.–Sun. 9am–7pm *This neoclassical church was built in 1783 by João Paulo in one of the oldest parts of Lisbon. It is not far from the Roman baths in Rua da Prata.*
■ **Chafariz de El-Rei (21)** Travessa Chafariz de El-Rei, 1100
One of the oldest fountains in the city, modified by Pombal in the 19th century.

■ Where to shop
➡ 132 ➡ 146

21

18

17

18

17

In the area

Standing some 1500 ft from the Castelo de São Jorge ➡ 90, outside the city walls, the Mosteiro de São Vicente de Fora and the Igreja de Santa Engrácia mark the northern limits of Alfama. Attracting fewer tourists, the area remains working-class and has wonderful views over the Tagus and

What to see

Mosteiro de São Vicente de Fora (22)
Largo de São Vicente, 1100 ☎ 888 56 52

🔲 12, tram 28 🕐 Tue.–Sun. 9am–1pm, 3–5pm ● no admission charge 📷

Perched on the hillside overlooking Alfama stands the impressive Mosteiro de São Vicente de Fora, erected in honor of the patron saint of Lisbon, São Vicente, to commemorate the battle of the Crusaders against the Moors. It was built between 1582 and 1627 by Filipo Terzi on the site of a 12th-century monastery and is without doubt one of the most impressive buildings in Lisbon. The plain façade of white limestone is of grandiose proportions and slightly stark in style, typical of Portuguese architecture of the 16th century. Built on a Latin cross plan, the church has a single nave and is highly decorated with baroque features, including an impressive mosaic of polychrome marble, a magnificent carved and gilded wooden altar screen (in the chapel of Our Lady of Pilar), and a wonderful parquet floor made of wood from Brazil (in the choir). The monastery is worth a visit if only to see the 18th-century panels of *azulejos* decorating the walls of the entrance hall and the Augustinian cloisters, offering a fine example of this decorative art that was so popular at the time. The panels depict both historical and country scenes, as well as some from La Fontaine's fables. At the back of the cloisters, the former refectory has been transformed into the Pantheon of the Bragança monarchs. ★ The first floor opens out onto a terrace which has wonderful views over the Tagus and the rooftops of Alfama.

Igreja de Santa Engrácia / Panteão Nacional (23)
Campo de Santa Clara, 1100

🔲 12, tram 28 🕐 Tue.–Sun. 10am–5pm; closed public holidays ● Esc. 250; under-25s and over-65s Esc. 125; under-14s free 📷

Started in 1681 by the architect João Antunes, the church was eventually completed in 1966! Built in the shape of a Greek cross and crowned with a dome (added in 1956), the church is a priceless example of Portuguese baroque architecture. The curves and counter-curves of pink and white marble covering the walls and floor create an amazing impression of space and movement, a feature which is typical of buildings dating from the reign of João V. Designated the national Pantheon, it contains six cenotaphs to the memory of famous historical names such as Vasco da Gama and Luís de Camões, as well as the tombs of former presidents and Portuguese celebrities. The body of Humberto Delgado, an opponent of the Salazar regime who was assassinated on the Spanish border on February 13, 1965, was moved here in 1990.

Not forgetting

■ **Museu Militar (24)** Largo do Museu da Artilharia, 1100 ☎ 886 21 31 🕐 Tue.–Sun. 10am–5pm; closed public holidays *A large collection of arms and ammunition, some of which dates from the 15th century, is displayed here in wonderful surroundings. The museum is decorated with carvings and paintings which date from the end of the 18th century and are also well worth seeing.*
■ **Campo de Santa Clara (25)** *This square brings together some beautiful 17th-century palaces and gardens in which the Feira da Ladra flea-market ➡ 146 is held every Tuesday and Saturday.*

the rooftops of Alfama.
- ■ Where to eat ➡ 24
- ■ After dark ➡ 70
- ■ Where to shop ➡ 146

When it was first built in the 16th century, the church of São Vicente de Fora in Alfama was outside the city walls.

As you follow the Tagus northward toward Expo '98, you come across the industrial district of Xábregas. Of little interest in itself, the area is worth visiting for the Madre de Deus monastery which contains some of the most beautiful *azulejos* in Portugal, including the superb pictorial

What to see

26

27

Museu Nacional do Azulejo (26)
4, rua da Madre de Deus, 1900 ☎ 814 77 47 ➠ 814 95 34

🚌 *104, 105* 🕐 *Tue. 2–6pm; Wed.–Sun. 10am–6pm* ● *Esc. 350; under-25s and over-65s, Esc. 125* 🔲 🍴 🛈 🔳

Azulejos form an integral part of the landscape of Portugal and Lisbon. They provide invaluable social and historical accounts of life in the past, and it is therefore not surprising that a special place has been dedicated to this art form, tracing its history and production. The museum, which opened in 1980 in the Madre de Deus monastery to the east of Lisbon, presents 500 years of *azulejo* art, which is exhibited in a chronological and educational way on two floors. This collection is the only one of its type in the world and contains thousands of examples of tiles, from Hispano-Moorish geometrical designs, tiles from Antwerp (16th-century), and baroque examples, to the most surprising contemporary work displayed at the end of the exhibit. The monastery and church also house a number of other pieces, notably the Nossa Senhora da Vida panel, a Portuguese mannerist *trompe-l'oeil* by Marçal de Matos, dating from around 1580. The most impressive exhibit, however, remains the 75ft-long panel showing Lisbon before the earthquake, from Xábregas to Cruz Quebrada. This can be viewed from the upper floor of the gallery which opens out to the grounds. A small restaurant, which is also decorated with *azulejos*, has been opened in what used to be the kitchens of the old monastery.

representation of
Lisbon before the
earthquake of 1755.

Igreja/Convento Madre de Deus (27)
4, rua da Madre de Deus, 1900 ☎ 814 77 47 ➡ 814 95 34

Entry via museum (see page 96 for prices and opening times)

Founded at the beginning of the 16th century by Dona Leonor (widow
of João II), this monastery run by Franciscan nuns is so luxurious that it
is more like a palace than the residence of a religious community. It
once contained many valuable paintings from Portuguese and Flemish
schools, but, like so many other buildings, did not withstand the
earthquake of 1755. Although the adjoining church was only partially
destroyed, it was decided to rebuild the whole complex in the 18th
century. Restored in 1981 with money from the Calouste Gulbenkian
Foundation, the church is a fine example of late 18th-century religious
architecture. The nave contains a feast of baroque *talhas douradas* (gilded
woodcarvings) which are perfectly complemented by the blue and white
Dutch *azulejos* from the 17th century. The crypt, in the form of a primitive
chapel, holds priceless tiles from Seville from the 16th century, but the
most impressive part of the church is the *corso alto* (gallery). This contains
the relics of Saint Just, an impressive coffered ceiling depicting scenes from
the life of the Virgin Mary, and a parquet floor made from exotic precious
woods. The few remaining traces of the original Manueline structure
(16th century) include the small cloisters of the monastery, decorated
with Moorish *azulejos*, and the external portal depicting a pelican and a
fishing net, symbols of Dona Leonor and João II.

In the area

This modern district, situated to the north of the Parque Eduardo VII ➡ 110 has, since the 19th century, been hemmed in by the large straight avenues known as the *avenidas novas*. Some old buildings have been saved here and there or have been incorporated into new ones. ■ Where to

What to see

Museu Calouste Gulbenkian (28)

45-A, avenida de Berna, 1067 ☎ 793 51 31 or 795 02 36 ➡ 795 52 49

Ⓜ *São Sebastião, Palhavã* 🕐 *daily 10am–5pm; closed public holidays* ● *Esc. 500; Sun., students and over-65s free* 🏛 🍴 🛈 💻

Calouste Gulbenkian, a rich American-born businessman and art lover, lived in Lisbon from 1942 until his death in 1955, collecting over 6000 works of art. In his will, he left money to establish the foundation that today carries his name. The buildings by the architects Alberto Pessoa, Ruy Athougia, and Pedro Cyd (based on designs by Gulbenkian himself) were not finished until 1969. A beautiful park, designed by Gonçalo Ribeiro Teles, surrounds the museum and contains a small lake, an amphitheater, and a number of modern sculptures scattered here and there. The museum exhibits collections of Egyptian, Assyrian, and Greek art and has an entire gallery devoted to Islamic art. Other rooms are reserved for the decorative arts and European paintings from the Middle Ages to the 18th century. ★ Of particular note is the area dedicated to the art-nouveau works of the jeweler and interior designer, René Lalique. Additional rooms are kept in reserve and are regularly used for temporary exhibitions.

Centro de Arte Moderna (29)

Rua Dr Nicolau de Bittencourt, 1067
☎ 793 51 31 or 795 02 41 ➡ 793 92 94

Ⓜ *São Sebastião, Palhavã* 🕐 *Tue., Thur., Fri., Sun. 10am–5pm; Wed., Sat. 10am–7pm; closed public holidays* ● *Esc. 500; Sun., under-14s, students, over-65s free*

Thanks to artists such as Pedro Cabrita Reis and Julião Sarmento, Portuguese art has been given a new lease of life since the 1974 Revolution. The Modern Art Museum, built in 1980 by the architect Sir Leslie Martin with the help of Ivor Richard Sommer Ribeiro, and Nunes Oliveira, is found in the grounds of the Calouste Gulbenkian Foundation. It traces the development of Portuguese painting from 1910 to the present day, reviewing all the modernist movements from its precursors Amadeo de Souza-Cardoso and Almada Negreiros, to the Abstract, Pop Art, and Minimalist movements which, in spite of the dictatorship and the enforced exile of many artists, still managed to retain a particular Portuguese flavor. The museum's rich archives are available for consultation by specialists.

Igreja de Nossa Senhora de Fátima (30)

Avenida Marquês de Tomar, 1050

Ⓜ *Campo Pequeno* 🕐 *daily 8.30am–1pm, 4.30–8pm* ● *no admission charge*

This church was designed by the architect Porfírio Pardal Monteiro. It was built between 1934 and 1938 and when it first opened was the source of much controversy among the less forward-looking of Lisbon society who were shocked by its modernist design. It was some time before this style of architecture became an accepted part of the religious buildings in Portugal. The interior is beautifully highlighted by the magnificent stained-glass windows by Almada Negreiros in both the choir (*O Calvário*) and the main chapel (*Anjos Cantores*).

The Calouste Gulbenkian Foundation regularly organizes open-air concerts ➡ 78.

In the area

Tourada (Portuguese bullfighting) unleashes the population's passions. When the bullfight ends, the bullrings empty and the party begins. Eating and drinking go on well into the night, accompanied by the sounds of *fados* telling of the most famous *cavaleiros*. ■ Where to stay ➡ 28.

➡ What to see

Praça de Touros de Campo Pequeno (31)
Avenida da República, 1050 ☎ 793 20 93 ➡ 793 21 91

Ⓜ *Campo Pequeno* 🕐 **Guided tours** Mon.–Fri. 9am–1pm, 2–6pm ● no admission charge touradas June–Oct.: from 10pm ● Esc. 2000–10,000 (entrance via gate 2 on Avenida da República) 🍴 🍺 open for touradas

The most famous Portuguese bullring is without doubt that at Campo Pequeno in Lisbon. Built in 1892 in a neo-Moorish style, it can hold 8000 spectators. *Tourada* is very different from its Spanish counterpart since the killing of bulls was banned in Portugal in 1933. Many of the *cavaleiros*, however, are used to killing bulls when performing in Spain but when Manuel dos Santos risked doing this at Campo Pequeno, bringing the bull down with his sword to the aghast cries of the crowd, he was immediately arrested and put in prison. Six bulls take part in each *tourada*, and for each bull there are two major events: one involving the *cavaleiros* and the other involving the *forcados* (stoppers). Dressed in richly embroidered costumes (the design of which dates back to the 17th century), the mounted *cavaleiro* enters the bullring. The agility of Portuguese horses is extremely impressive. The rider and his mount execute a number of passes (*sortes*) sticking banderillas into the neck of the bull. In Portugal, audience participation is an integral part of the show with each pass by the *cavaleiro* being punctuated by loud whistles and clapping. The best *cavaleiros* are those who are able to make the passes while

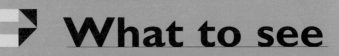

Av.Á.Pais   ENTRE CAMPOS
R.Dr.E.Neves
R.de Entrecampos
Av.A.Serpa   Campo Pequeno   Av. S. Cabral
Cinco de Outubro
Av.J.Dinis   **31**   R.Ó.M.Torres
Avenida da República
Campo Pequeno
39
Av. de Berna   Campo Pequeno   Av. João XXI
Ⓜ Campo Pequeno
Avenida   Avenida da   Barbosa du Bocage

remaining calmly in control and allowing the bull to come as near to
them as possible. João Moura is one of the most famous and, like many
other *cavaleiros*, he also performs in Spain and South America. If the
tourada was originally an aristocratic sport (as suggested by the noble
fight of the *cavaleiro*), that of the *pega* is the continuation of a working-
class tradition that dates back two centuries. At that time, the *pega*
took place in public squares where men with *forcados* (long curved sticks)
were in charge of preventing the animal from escaping. Spectacular
to watch, this is the event that Portuguese spectators enjoy the most.
Eight *forcados* line up in front of the bull, defiantly staring at it and ready
to stop it if it charges at them. On a signal, the first *forcado* throws
himself at the animal, taking hold of its neck, while two more *forcados*
grab its horns. The others gather round and try to stop the bull from
moving, forcing its head down. The last one grabs hold of its tail. The bull
must be pulled to the ground within seconds. Even though the horns
are covered with leather sheaths, the exercise
is still extremely dangerous. In the last century,
the *pega* was actually banned for some time
following the deaths of two *forcados*. However,
as a result of public pressure, the ban was
soon lifted. It is truly with the *pega* that
Portuguese bullfighting sets itself apart
from similar bullfighting sports in
other countries.

From the pretty area of Lapa, walk along Rua de São Domingos then Rua de Buenos Aires to the Jardim da Estrela, opposite the basilica. Further on is Campo Ourique, a lively village-like area. ■ Where to stay ➡ 24 ➡ 30 ■ Where to eat ➡ 44 ➡ 46 ➡ 48 ■ After dark ➡ 68 ➡ 70 ➡ 72

What to see

Museu Nacional de Arte Antiga (32)
9, rua das Janelas Verdes, 1200 ☎ 396 41 51

🚋 tram 15, 18 🕐 Tue. 2–6pm; Wed.–Sun. 10am–6pm ● Esc. 500; under-25s and over-65s Esc. 250 📕 🎫 🏠 📺 📷

Built in the 12th century on the site of the former St Albert monastery, this palace was originally owned by the first Count Alvor and later belonged to the Marquês de Pombal. In 1882, an exhibition of ornamental art was held here, focusing people's attention on the issue of the country's artistic heritage. Two years later, it was decided to turn this palace into the National Museum of Fine Art and Archeology, which became the Museu Nacional de Arte Antiga in 1911. Its various collections, exhibited on three levels, make it the largest in Portugal.
Level One contains objets d'art from the 15th to the 17th centuries and has a section devoted to foreign paintings with works by Italian, French, German, Flemish, and Spanish masters. The prize exhibit remains the triptych by Jerome Bosch, *The Temptation of Saint Anthony*, one of the artist's later works.
Level Two is entirely devoted to gold and silver religious objects and a collection of oriental decorative arts from former Portuguese colonies. The latter contains examples of Indo-Portuguese and Namban art, including an incredible collection of Japanese screens depicting the departure from Goa and the arrival of the Portuguese in Nagasaki in 1543.
Level Three traces the history of Portuguese painting from the Middle Ages to the 19th century. This is where you will find the world-famous polyptych of Saint Vincent (1460). Discovered in the attics of São Vicente de Fora ➡ 94 in 1882, this painting is believed to be by Nuno Gonçalves and is a priceless record of Lisbon society in the 15th century. All the main characters are present (Afonso V and Prince Henry the Navigator) as well as members of all the social classes. ★ A viewing platform in the adjoining garden offers a wonderful view over the port ➡ 112.

Not forgetting

■ **Palácio Real das Necessidades (33)** Largo do Rilvas, 1300 *Built in 1742, this palace withstood the earthquake and was a royal residence until 1910. Today it houses the government department in charge of foreign affairs and is no longer open to visitors. It has a wonderful view over the Tagus.*
■ **Casa de Fernando Pessoa (34)** 16, rua Coelho da Rocha, 1250 ☎ 396 81 90 or 396 81 99 ➡ 396 82 62 🕐 Mon.–Wed., Fri.–Sun. 1–6pm; Thur. 1–8pm *The house where the poet spent the last 15 years of his life. It has since been modernized and is now used as the Casa da Poesia. Pessoa's personal library has been preserved here as well as some of his works. There is a café in the inner courtyard ➡ 78.*
■ **Basílica da Estrela (35)** Praça da Estrela, 1200 🕐 daily 7am–1pm, 3–8pm *Built in 1779–90, it has an impressive façade with two towers and a dome from where you can enjoy a breathtaking view over the whole of Lisbon.*
■ **Fundação Árpad Szenes – Vieira da Silva (36)** 56–58, praça das Amoreiras, 1250 🕐 Mon., Wed.–Sat. noon–8pm; Sun. 10am–6pm; closed public holidays *Housed in a former silk factory and opened to the public in 1995, the foundation presents the work of Vieira da Silva and her husband Árpad Szenes as well as holding temporary exhibitions devoted to the monuments associated with them.*

➡ 76 ➡ 78
■ Where to
shop ➡ 130
➡ 140

Casa de
Fernando Pessoa
has permanent
exhibitions and
hosts cultural
events ➡ 78.

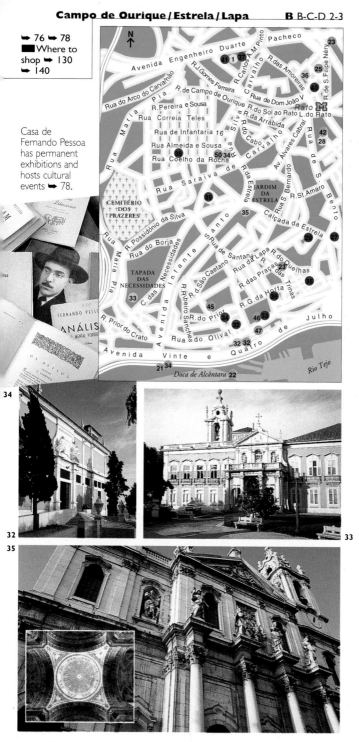

In the area

The monuments of Belém commemorate the Age of Discoveries and the great Portuguese explorers. This pleasant residential area is the official home of the President of Portugal. ■ Where to eat ➡ 52 ➡ 54 ■ After dark ➡ 78 ■ What to see ➡ 110 ■ Where to shop ➡ 144

What to see

Torre de Belém (37)

🚇 43, tram 15 🕐 Tue.–Sun. 10am–5pm ● *Esc. 400; young person's discount card, students, over-65s Esc. 200* 📋

Built in the middle of the Tagus in 1515 to defend the mouth of the river, the Torre de Belém was joined to the mainland by a sandbank caused by the tidal wave that followed the earthquake of 1755. One of the most famous monuments in Portugal and an unusual example of military architecture. The work of Francisco de Arruda, the tower has five floors and a terrace on the top with spectacular views over the Tagus. It is typical of Manueline architecture that was popular at the time, with its Venetian-style galleries and Moorish domes.

Padrão dos Descobrimentos (38)
Avenida de Brasília, 1400

🚇 43, tram 15 🕐 Tue.–Sun. 9.30am–7pm; closed public holidays ● **viewing platform** *Esc. 320; young person's discount card, students Esc. 160; under-12s free ● **Exhibitions** no admission charge* 🍴 🔲

Erected in 1960 to commemorate the 500th anniversary of the death of Prince Henry the Navigator, this tribute to the Age of Discoveries is typical of the style that was popular under the Salazar regime. The term *padrão* recalls the posts erected by Portuguese explorers in the new territories they had discovered. At the front of the bows of this caravel, made of reinforced concrete and covered with pink stone from Leiria, stands the statue of Prince Henry followed by 32 other figures carved by Leopoldo de Almeida, António Santos, and Soares Branco. ★ An elevator takes you to a viewing platform from where you have a wonderful view of the compass, some 150ft in diameter, laid out on the ground in front of the monument. In the center, a planisphere retraces the main routes taken by Portuguese explorers. Inside there are temporary exhibitions.

Museu Nacional dos Coches (39)
Praça Afonso de Albuquerque, 1300 ☎ 361 08 50 ➠ 363 72 46

🚇 43, tram 15 🕐 Tue.–Sun. 10am–6pm ● *Esc. 450* 🔲

This is the most visited museum in Lisbon. The former riding school of the royal palace of Belém now houses many coaches and carriages of all kinds that were once used by royal and noble households, along with harnesses, emblems, ceremonial uniforms, and other paraphernalia connected with horse-riding.

Not forgetting

■ **Museu de Arte Popular (40)** Avenida de Brasília, 1400 ☎ 301 12 81 🕐 Tue.–Sun. 10am–5pm *An exhibition of traditional Portuguese costumes, crafts, and furniture.* ■ **Centro Cultural de Belém (41)** Praça do Império, 1400 ☎ 361 24 00 ➠ 361 25 00 🕐 **Exhibitions** daily 11am–8pm *Built in 1992 by Vittorio Gregotti and Manuel Salgado, this is the only large new building project undertaken in the capital since the revolution of April 25, 1974. It includes auditoriums, studios, galleries, and a park in which exhibitions of contemporary sculptures are held* ➡ 78.

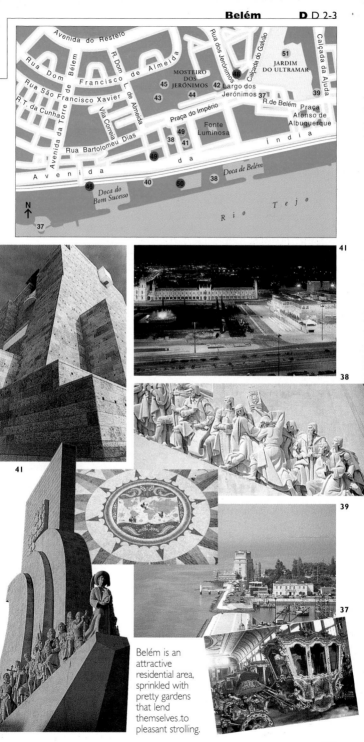

51 JARDIM DO ULTRAMAR

Avenida do Restelo

Rua Dom de Belém

Rua Dom L. de Almeida

R. Dom

Francisco de Almeida

Rua São Francisco Xavier

R.T. da Cunhe

Avenida da Torre de Belém

Vila Correia

Rua dos Jerónimos

Calçada do Galvão

Calçada da Ajuda

MOSTEIRO DOS JERÓNIMOS

48

45

42 Largo dos Jerónimos

43

44

37

39

R. de Belém

Praça Afonso de Albuquerque

Praça do Império

Fonte Luminosa

Rua Bartolomeu Dias

49

38 41

49

d a Í n d i a

A v e n i d a

Doca de Belém

46

Doca do Bom Sucesso

40

50

38

N

37

R i o   T e j o

41

38

39

37

41

Belém is an attractive residential area, sprinkled with pretty gardens that lend themselves to pleasant strolling.

The Age of Discoveries gave rise, during the reign of Manuel I, to a style of architecture that became known in the 19th century as Manueline. It can be recognized by the use of stone ornamentation incorporating marine and floral motifs inspired by distant civilizations. The Mosteiro dos Jerónimos and the tower of Bélim ➡ 52 are the best examples of this style.

What to see

Mosteiro dos Jerónimos (42)
Praça do Império, 1400 ☎ 362 00 34 or 362 00 38 ➡ 363 91 45

▣ 43, 27, 49, 51, 28, tram 15 ◷ Tue.–Sun. 10am–5pm ● Esc. 400; young person's discount card, students, under-65s Esc. 200 ▣ ▦

This masterpiece of Manueline architecture was built between 1517 and 1522 at the request of Manuel I on the site of a small chapel founded in 1496 by Prince Henry the Navigator, Master of the Order of Christ. It is said that Vasco da Gama came here to pray on the eve of his expedition to the Indies. The spice trail proved to be the source of inestimable wealth and it was this money that made it possible to carry out such a project, symbolizing the glory and power of Portugal during the Age of Discoveries. This impressive monument was originally built in Gothic style (under the supervision of Boytac) and was then decorated with the rich Manueline ornamentation that has made it so famous. The Spanish-born João de Castilho added a Plateresque touch, Nicolas Chanterene introduced the major themes of the Renaissance, and then, in the 19th century, Diego de Torralva and Jérôme de Rouen brought classical features to the west wing that now houses the Museum of Archeology. The southern portal (the work of Boytac and João de Castilho) takes you to the Igreja Santa Maria and is decorated with statuettes and marine motifs and topped with a canopy bearing the cross of the Knights of Christ. The central nave of the church is 300ft long and 75ft high and is supported by six octagonal pillars decorated with Renaissance motifs which contrast sharply with the baroque style adopted by Jérôme de Rouen in the transept. When you consider how delicate the pillars look, it seems incredible that the ribbed vaulting in the nave, the work of João de Castilho, was able to withstand the earthquake of 1755. The more classical choir of the church (added in 1571–2, then rebuilt in the 17th century) contains some surprising sarcophagi carried by elephants. Eminent members of the Aviz dynasty (including Manuel I) lie here. The corso alto (gallery) is decorated with stalls and paneling in maple and houses the neo-Manueline tombs of Vasco da Gama and Luís de Camões. From here, you also have views over the whole of the impressive nave. Entrance to the cloisters is via the west portal which also serves as the main entrance to the church and is decorated with statues of King Manuel and Queen Maria. The cloisters are an architectural jewel, lined with large late-baroque and Renaissance arcades. The window in the chapter house and its two posts covered with sculptures is world famous as one of the finest examples of Manueline architecture.

Not forgetting
■ **Museu da Marinha (43)** Praça do Império, 1400 ☎ 362 00 19 ➡ 363 19 87 ◷ Tue.–Sun. 10am–5pm Model sets tell the story of the history Portuguese navigation. Entrance is via the west wing of the monastery. ■ **Museu de Arqueologia (44)** Praça do Império, 1400 ☎ 362 00 00 ➡ 362 00 16 ◷ Tue. 2–6pm; Wed.–Sun. 10am–6pm Situated in the west wing of the Mosteiro dos Jerónimos, the museum has Egyptian, Roman, and Lusitanian artifacts. ■ **Planetário Gulbenkian (45)** Praça do Império, 1400 ☎ 362 00 02 ➡ 363 60 05 ◷ Sat., Sun. at 4pm and 5pm Opened in 1965, it is money from the Gulbenkian Foundation has financed the technical equipment used to recreate the movement of the stars.

North of the Parque Florestal de Monsanto are the northernmost outskirts of Lisbon, a neglected area. The park itself is crossed by a number of roads and you are advised to avoid it late at night. ■ Where to stay ➡ 30 ■ Where to eat ➡ 46 ➡ 48 ➡ 54 ➡ 56 ■ After dark

➡ What to see

Parque Florestal de Monsanto (46)

🖼 2, 13, 24 🕐 open every day ● no admission charge 🎏 🍸 🖵

Created in 1934 by Salazar, the Parque Florestal is truly the green heart of Lisbon. Planted with eucalyptus, oak, plane, and cedar, following the plans of Duarte Pacheco, the park covers such a vast area that certain parts have been neglected. ★ A telescope from the panoramic restaurant of Monsanto enables you to see the south bank of the Tagus, the Ponte 25 de Abril ➡ 112, and the statue of Cristo Rei ➡ 112. Montes Claros rises to 700ft and is a beautiful spot complete with a small lake and wonderful plants.

Palácio Marquês da Fronteira (47)
Largo São Domingos de Benfica, 1500 ☎ 778 20 23 ➡ 778 49 62

🖼 72 🕐 June–Sep.: Mon.–Sat. 10.30am, 11am, 11.30am, noon; Oct.–May: Mon.–Sat. 11am, noon; closed public holidays ● **Palace and garden** Mon.–Fri. Esc. 1100; Sat. Esc. 1500 ● **Garden** Mon.–Fri. Esc. 300; Sat. Esc. 500 🎫 only

Situated on the northern edge of the park close to Benfica, this 17th-century hunting lodge, built by João Mascarenhas, is outstanding because of the number of different azulejos used to decorate both the interior and exterior. In the small French-style garden, the blue façade of the king's gallery forms a shaded terrace, reflected in a small ornamental lake, and is decorated with the busts of 15 Portuguese monarchs. Below, a series of arched panels depict the Mascarenhas family. The highlight of any visit is the small cave, the Casa de Fresco, decorated with mother-of-pearl, ceramics, and pieces of Chinese porcelain. The walls of the palace are decorated with a number of surprising illustrations: angels, demons, cats and monkeys with disconcertingly human expressions.

Aqueduto das Águas Livres (48)

🎫 contact the Museu da Água ☎ 813 55 22

Built between 1729 and 1749 on the orders of João V to supply the city with water, the aqueduct is almost 40 miles long and runs above the north of Lisbon and the Parque de Monsanto. It carries water as far as the Mãe d'Água (Mother of Waters), Lisbon's main reservoir at Praça das Amoreiras. The largest of its arches, at Campolide, is 210ft high. ★ A pleasant walk under the arches decorated with azulejos will take you as far as the Parque Florestal de Monsanto.

Not forgetting

■ **Palácio da Ajuda (49)** Calçada da Ajuda, 1300 ☎ 363 70 95 ➡ 364 82 23 🕐 Mon., Tue., Thur.–Sun. 10am–5pm; closed public holidays *The Palácio da Ajuda was once a royal residence, begun in 1802 during the reign of João VI but never completed due to the arrival of Napoleon's troops. Some 20 years later, Dom Miguel won the battle for the crown and proclaimed himself absolute monarch in 1828. This classical palace today houses the Ministry of Culture and a museum which boasts the dinner service used by the kings of Portugal, made by the French goldsmith Germain-Thomas. It is one of the few European royal services to remain completely intact.*

➡ 68 ➡ 78 ▬
What to see ➡ 102
➡ 110 ▬ Where
to shop ➡ 130

The charming Palácio Marquês da Fronteira, which was built in the 17th century, is well known for its beautiful gardens that are adorned with a variety of *azulejos*.

Bougainvillea, lemon trees, jacarandas, nettle trees and many other species are found on the streets, stone walls and courtyards. Around the palaces, French and English-style gardens or botanical gardens have been established with plants from former colonies. Lisbon has many acres of parkland providing wide open spaces through which to enjoy a stroll.

What to see

Parque Eduardo VII (50)

Ⓜ *Rotunda* ◯ **Park** *open all hours;* **Greenhouses** *daily 9am–4.30pm*
● *Esc. 95*

These French-style gardens, opened in 1902 to commemorate the visit of the British monarch, cover an area just beyond Praça Marquês de Pombal. From the viewing platform at the top end of the park you can see the district of Baixa, the port ➡ 112, and the opposite bank of the Tagus. On the northwestern side is the Estufa Fria, a greenhouse built in the 1930s by Raul Carapinha. Covering around 50 acres, it contains a forest of tropical flowers and plants, interspersed with waterfalls and small Japanese bridges. On the eastern side of the park stands the Pavilhão dos Desportos. The façade of this baroque pavilion is covered with wonderful panels of *azulejos* depicting historical scenes. ★ The park also has an area for concerts, exhibitions, and theatrical productions.

Jardim do Ultramar (51)
Calçada do Galvão, 1400 ☎ 363 70 23

🚌 *28, 27, 49, tram 15* ◯ *Tue.–Sun. 10am–5pm; closed public holidays* ● *Esc. 100*

Built in 1906 by Manuel Antonio Moreira Junior, the park has been known over the years as the Jardim Tropical, the Jardim Colonial, and the Jardim do Ultramar. Containing plants from the former Portuguese colonies of Angola, Mozambique, and Brazil, the gardens have, since 1912, occupied 700 acres of what used to be the grounds of the Palace of Belém. The 17th-century Palácio do Patio das Vacas now houses a museum containing a wonderful collection of 16–19th-century *azulejos*, over 3000 woodcuts from all over the world, a herbarium of plants from former Portuguese colonies, and numerous works of art from African countries that were once part of the Portuguese Empire. At present closed to the public, it is due to reopen in time for Expo '98.

Jardim Botânico (52)
58, rua da Escola Politécnica, 1500 ☎ 396 15 21 ➡ 397 08 82

🚌 *58, 100* ◯ *winter: daily 9am–6pm; summer: daily 9am–8pm; closed Christmas and New Year* ● *Esc. 200; children free*

This is one of the largest collections of subtropical vegetation in Europe. Set in an area of naturally undulating ground, the pathways guide the visitor around man-made lakes, up specially constructed staircases, over bridges, and past sculptures. The gardens are part of the science faculty which also houses a museum of science and natural history.

Not forgetting

■ **Jardim Zoológico (53)** 158–160, estrada de Benfica, 1500 ☎ 726 93 49 ➡ 726 47 73 ◯ *winter; daily 10am–6pm; summer: daily 10am–8pm. The upper part has been left wild, perfect for a walk or picnic in the open. Around a lake lies a rose garden and a zoo. From the cable car, you have a breathtaking view over the zoo and city. Various educational talks and exhibitions on the animals are organized throughout the year.*

In the area

The Tagus rises in Spain and travels over 500 miles to join the ocean off the coast of Portugal, forming an estuary to the southeast of Lisbon. It has been nicknamed *Mar de Palha*, the Sea of Straw, because of its yellowish color. The harbor was for many years the heart of the city.

What to see

Porto de Lisboa (54)

Lisbon has always looked toward the sea, turning its back on the old continent. Its strategic position at the mouth of the Tagus has made it the envy of its neighbors. The port played an important part in Lisbon's economy during the Age of Discoveries and the days of the empire. Over the centuries, it continued to grow in importance until it became one of the major ports-of-call in Europe, covering an area of over 12 miles along the banks of the Tagus. Today, however, it is used by far fewer ships and so some parts have been redeveloped in order to keep them viable. Over the past few years, restaurants, bars, and nightclubs have brought new life to these former docks. Redevelopment projects, aimed at making the river a more prominent feature of the town, have led to the creation of parks with views over the opposite banks and the building of small marinas and beaches at Costa de Caparica ➡ 124. From the dockside, ferries leave regularly for Barreiro, Montijo, Seixal, Cacilhas, Porto Brandão, and Trafaria. Not far from Cais das Colunas (dock of columns), you will find the art deco station (1931) of the Cais do Sodré railroad company, the harbor station of Rocha do Conde de Óbidos (1943), used in summer by pleasure cruisers (it contains paintings by Almada Negreiros), and the former power station dating from 1909 and now home of the Museum of Electricity.

Ponte 25 de Abril (55)

🕐 *24 hrs a day* ● **bridge for vehicular traffic** *Esc.100 per car*

The people of Lisbon had always wanted a bridge linking the two banks of the Tagus and in 1959 Portugal organized an international competition to design such a link. The winner was the United States Steel Export company. When building work began in 1962, the main aim was to enable the beaches of the south coast to be developed. Over a mile long, this suspension bridge, linking Alcântara to the left bank, was at the time of its completion the longest in Europe. Originally named the Ponte Salazar, it became known as the Ponte 25 de Abril following the Captain's Revolution in 1974. The bridge becomes heavily congested during rush hour (used by around 600 million vehicles each year) and it is unfortunately not possible to stop to admire the unforgettable view of the estuary. The bridge itself can be seen from various viewing platforms that are scattered around the city.

Cristo Rei (56)
Alto do Pregal, 2800 Almada

🕐 *winter: daily 9am–6.30pm; summer: daily 9am–8pm* ● **elevator** *Esc. 200; under-8s free*

Built between 1947 and 1949, this obelisk (the work of the sculptor Francisco Franco) is topped with a replica of the statue of Christ the Redeemer that overlooks Rio de Janeiro and was allegedly erected to thank God for having spared Lisbon during World War II. The base is 270ft high and the statue rises a further 90ft. An elevator takes you to a viewing platform from where you have a breathtaking view over the city and the Tagus. On a clear day, you can even make out the Arrábida Peninsula as far as Setúbal ➡ 124.

56

54

The new Ponte Vasco da Gama (below), situated northeast of Lisbon, spans the 988 acres of salt marshes of Samouco, refuge to a number of species of migratory birds ➡ 114.

54

Expo '98, which takes place from May 22 to September 30, is the 100th international exhibition to be held since the Great Exhibition in London in 1851. Expo '98 is based around the theme of the Oceans, marking the 500th anniversary of Vasco da Gama's expedition to India. It has brought about the creation of a new center in Lisbon and marks

Expo '98

Expo '98 (57)

🅼 *Oriente* 🕙 *9am–3am* @ *http://www.expo98.pt* 📺 *0808 209 898 (from Portugal)* ● *Day pass: Esc. 5000; 5–14s, over 65s: Esc. 2500; 3-day pass: Esc. 12 500; 5–14s and over 65s: Esc. 6250; "Expo Noite" pass (valid from 8pm–3am): one price of Esc. 2000.* ☎ *86 80 426 for groups* ➡ *86 81 800* @ *ticketing@expo98.pt*

Pavilhão de Portugal

The Pavilion of Portugal, located in the middle of the exhibition on the Doca dos Olivais and capable of welcoming up to 20,000 visitors each day, is the work of the architect Álvaro Siza Vieira. Its theme: an historical and interactive exhibition (designed by the architect Eduardo Souto Moura under the direction of the art historian Simonetta Lux Afonso) on the history of navigation and the discovery of new cultures. It aims to recreate the voyage of Vasco da Gama, who reached the coast of India in May 1498. Close to the pavilion stands a covered area where ceremonies will be held to mark the national holidays of each of the 132 participating countries.

Area Internacional

The international exhibition of 1998 is especially innovative in the way the countries taking part are represented. Rather than having an area in which to build their own stand, the organizers have given them each a unit in the great hall in which to present their own interpretation of the theme "The Oceans, a heritage for the future". The 40 main participating countries are located in the southern part of the hall in stands of between 1 and 5 units (each of about 16 square yards) arranged around four interior squares. After Expo '98, this hall will become an exhibition center to replace the old Feira Internacional de Lisboa, situated close to the Ponte de 25 Abril.

Pavilhão dos Oceanos

Designed by the American architect Peter Chermayeff, this giant aquarium (the largest in Europe) consists of a central tank containing some 5500 cubic yards of seawater (equivalent to four Olympic-size swimming

The sketches of the Portuguese Pavilion by Álvaro Siza Vieira show the enormous sail rising daringly above its two supports.

the starting point for one of the largest urban redevelopment projects in Europe. It has also led to the city reclaiming the areas to the east situated along the river which were until recently occupied by docks and refineries.

pools) that recreates the high seas, including fishes, from sardines to sharks. Four smaller aquaria (Antarctic, Indian Ocean, North Pacific and the Azores) complete this peninsula-shaped building.

Pavilhão da Utopia

The Utopia Pavilion presents a show entitled "Oceanos e Utopias", drawing on theater, light shows, optical effects and the latest multimedia technology. After the exhibition has finished, this pavilion, with seating for 15,000, will be used to stage various types of entertainment.

Pavilhão do Conhecimento dos Mares

At the center of this project, the Pavilion of Knowledge of the Seas is the work of the architect Carrilho da Graça. It features a huge ship being built in a shipyard. With simplified scientific and technological explanations, it traces the development of maritime exploration and invention through the ages.

Pavilhão do Futuro

The Pavilion of the Future, built by three leading Portuguese architects, Santos, Ramos and Guedes, completes the central message of Expo '98 with its celebration of the Oceans as the heritage of future generations. The focal point of this exhibit is a multimedia show in 3D.

Estação do Oriente

Situated not far from the entrance to the exhibition, this new integrated station will become the focal point of the transport network serving Lisbon and its surroundings, including a station for intercity and commuter trains, a subway station, a bus depot and a link with Lisbon's international airport. The building itself, with a roof of glass and steel made to look like a row of trees, is the work of the Spanish architect and engineer Santiago Calatrava, the designer of such spectacular constructions as the station of Lyons-Satolas in France.

Ponte Vasco da Gama

The building of a second crossing over the "sea of straw" was considered to be vitally important in the development of Lisbon and its surroundings. This bridge has been the subject of controversy, not least because of the choice of route through the ecologically sensitive area of the Tagus estuary, close to the Benavente nature reserve for migrating birds, and because of the involvement of international civil engineering consortiums in a project financed by the EU.

Further afield

Guided tours
Gray Line ☎ 352 25 94
Portugal Tours ☎ 316 03 99
🕐 dep. daily at 2.30pm from
Av. Sidónio Pais; lasts approx.
5 hours ● 8000 Esc.
Cityrama ☎ 319 10 90
🕐 dep. daily at 9am from
Av. Sidónio Pais; lasts approx.
9 hours ● Esc. 11,000,
Esc. 13,000 with lunch

Costa da Caparica

In summer (Jun. 1–Sep. 30), a small train travels along the coast between the bridge and Fonte de Telha, serving all the beaches (19 stops!).

◯ *9am–7pm; dep. every 20 mins* ● *Esc. 200–Esc. 350 single and Esc. 350–Esc. 550 return, depending on the length of the journey*

13
Days out

THE INSIDER'S FAVORITES

Beaches

Being on the coast, Lisbon is within easy reach of a large number of beaches. Many are less than 20 miles form the center of the city and are very popular with those living in Lisbon.

To the west:
Estoril and Cascais (17 miles away), the most popular resorts.

To the northwest:
Praia do Guincho (22 miles away), a surfer's paradise; Praia da Roca (28 miles away), after a visit to Sintra; Praia Grande and Praia das Maças (30 miles away), very popular.

To the south:
Praia da Caparica (5–10 miles away), huge beach with dunes; Baia de Setúbal (20–30 miles away), remote beaches and charming little resorts.

Imagine the mildest of climates, lush exotic vegetation, a landscape of hills and forests crossed by paths and scattered here and there with charming little *quintas;* then imagine the sea, fishing villages, huge sand dunes, coastal resorts, rugged creeks and the most westerly point in Europe... and you are beginning to get a picture of the Costa de Lisboa.

◢ Further afield

Estoril (1)

15 miles west of Lisbon

➘ dep. Cais do Sodré every 20 mins, takes 30 mins

● Esc. 185

🚗 follow the A5 or the N6 (known as the Marginal)

Tourist office
Arcadas do Parque, 2765 Estoril
☎ (01) 466 38 13

Cascais (2)

17 miles west of Lisbon

➘ dep. Cais do Sodré every 15 mins, takes 20 mins

● Esc. 185

🚗 see Estoril

Tourist office
Rua Visconde de Luz, 2750 Cascais
☎ (01) 484 40 86

Queluz (3)

8 miles west of Lisbon

➘ dep.Cais do Sodré every 15 mins, takes 20 mins

● Esc. 100

🚗 follow the IC 19

Tourist office
see Sintra

Sintra (4)

16 miles north-west of Lisbon

➘ dep. Cais do Sodré, every 15 mins, takes 45 mins

● Esc. 185

🚗 follow IC 19

Tourist office
Praça da Republica, 2710 Sintra
☎ (01) 923 11 57

Costa de Caparica (5)

3-6 miles south of Lisbon

🚌 dep. Entre Campos Pr. da Areeiro or Pr. de Espanha every 20 mins takes 30 mins

● Esc. 400, 360, 290

⛴ dep. Cais do Sodré for Cacilhas or Belém for Trafaria every 20 mins, then a bus ride takes 30 or 40 mins depending on the journey

● Esc. 280 and Esc. 400

🚗 leave Lisbon by the Ponte 25 de Abril (A2), then follow the main road

Tourist office
18, Avenida da República, 2825

Costa de Caparica
☎ (01) 290 00 71

Cabo Espichel (6)

24 miles south of Lisbon

🚌 dep. Pr. de Espanha at 1.40pm and 2.50pm takes 30 mins

● Esc. 285

🚗 leave Lisbon by the Ponte 25 de Abril (A2), then take the N378 followed by N379

Tourist office (at Sesimbra)
26-27, Largo da Marinha, 2970 Sesimbra
☎ (01) 223 57 43

Sesimbra (7)

19 miles south of Lisbon

🚌 dep. Pr. de Espanha every 1 1/2 hours, takes 1 hour

● Esc. 500

🚗 leave Lisbon by the Ponte 25 de Abril (A2), then take the N378

Tourist office
26-27, Largo da Marinha, 2970 Sesimbra
☎ (01) 223 57 43

Vila Fresca de Azeitão (8) Quinta de Bacalhoa (9)

19 and 20 miles south of Lisbon

🚌 dep. Pr. da Espanha every 30 mins, takes 1 hour

● Esc. 500

🚗 take the Ponte 25 de Abril (A2) then head for Setúbal on the N10

Tourist office
Praça do Quebedo, 2900 Setúbal
☎ (065) 53 42 22

Setúbal (10)

27 miles south-east of Lisbon

➘ dep. Cais do Sodré every 30 mins, takes 30 mins

● Esc. 250

🚌 dep. Pr. de Espanha every 15 mins, takes 25 mins

● Esc. 500

🚗 take the Ponte 25 de Abril (A2) then the N10

Tourist office
Praça do Quebedo, 2900 Setúbal
☎ (065) 53 42 22

4   2   1

Rio Tejo

N 1

N 10

N 118

N 10

Ericeira 12

Mafra 11

N 247

N 9

A 8

A 9

A 1

N 117

lares

Sintra 4

IC 19

Queluz 3

✈

LISBOA

Montijo ○

N 4

A 5

1 Estoril

N 6

2

Cascais

Rio Tejo

Almada ○

Barreiro ○

Costa da Caparica 5

N 10

A 2

N 378

Bacalhoa 9

Vila Fresca de Azeitão 8

10

Setúbal

SERRA DA ARRÁBIDA

N 379

Santana ○

7 Sesimbra

6 Cabo Espichel

Mafra (11)

27 miles north-west of Lisbon

🚌 dep. Campo Grande every hour; takes 1 hour
● Esc. 510
🚗 take the A 8 then the N116 or the IC19 then the N117 and N9
Tourist office
Avenida 25 de Abril, 2640 Mafra
☎ (061) 81 20 23

Ericeira (12)

31 miles north-west of Lisbon

🚌 dep. Campo Grande, every hour takes 1 hour 20 mins ● Esc. 600
🚗 take the A 8

then the N116, or the IC19 then the N247
Tourist office
Rua Mendes Leal, 2655 Ericeira
☎ (061) 631 22

Colares (13)

21 miles north-west of Lisbon

🚌 dep. from Sintra, every 30 mins
● Esc. 250
🚗 from Sintra take the N247 or follow the coast via Cascais (N6 then N247)
Tourist office
see Sintra

11

6

5

A short journey along the coast takes you to the two most popular resorts around Lisbon: Estoril and Cascais. Beyond the rather unattractive outskirts of the city, both road and rail take you past the large Tagus estuary, beaches, coves, and beautiful *quintas*. From São João, take time to enjoy a picturesque walk along the seafront.

Further afield

Estoril (1)

Since the 18th century, the 'town where spring comes twice' has been attracting visitors to its mild climate and thermal waters. Estoril became famous when Queen Maria Pia de Sabóia, already a devotee of Cascais, chose to spend her summer vacations on the beaches of São João, São Pedro, and Monte Estoril. This choice was later shared by a stream of deposed kings, pretenders to the thrones of Europe, rich businessmen, spies, and World War I refugees. The old **casino**, once a focal point of this cosmopolitan and fashionable town, still attracts players to its tables today. Built overlooking the sea, the **Igreja de Santo António** is a former Franciscan monastery well worth a visit for its 17th- and 18th-century *talhas* (gilded woodcuts) that come from the Santa Marta monastery in Lisbon, and for its beautiful collection of blue and white *azulejos* dating from the same period. Nowadays, a number of other attractions ensure Estoril's continued fame: the impressive **golf course** on the outskirts of the town, the **Portuguese Grand Prix** which takes place on the racing circuit to the north, and the **Portuguese Open Tennis Championships**. In contrast, the neighboring resort of Cascais has succeeded in maintaining a more traditional atmosphere.

Cascais (2)

Already a sizeable fishing town during the reign of Afonso Henriques (12th century) and completely rebuilt after the earthquake of 1755, Cascais became truly established in the 19th century with the building of numerous **old style summer residences**: the palace of the Palmela family designed by the architect Thomas Wyatt, and that of the Loulés (nicknamed the 'box of almonds' and now housing the Albatroz Hotel) by Caetano Pedro d'Ávila; **more modern palaces** such as that of the counts of Castro Guimarães by Francisco Vilaça, and the **typical Portuguese houses** such as the Santa Maria *solar* (villa) by the architect Raul Lino. The **fortress** dominating the Bay of Cascais was partly destroyed by the Duke of Alva in 1580 and rebuilt in the 17th century. In the **citadel** you can visit the retreat of Nossa Senhora da Vitória with its baroque *talha* and 18th-century *azulejos*. Close by, the former **Convento dos Capuchinhos** (Capuchin monastery) which has now been transformed into an art center, contains a statue of the poet Camões by João Cutileiro. A number of churches are also of interest: the **Igreja Nossa Senhora da Assunção** with its collection of paintings (works by Josefa de Óbidos, 17th century, depicting the life of Saint Teresa of Avila, and paintings on wood by the Master of Lourinhã, 16th century), the **Igreja Nossa Senhora dos Navegantes**, the octagonal plan of which is a fine example of the baroque style of architecture from the reign of João V, and the **Igreja da Misericórdia** containing five mannerist paintings on wood by Cristóvão Vaz, a local artist whose works can also be found in the **Nossa Senhora do Guia**, a Manueline chapel on the way to the **Boca do Inferno** (a deep gorge in the side of the cliff where waves smash against each other), the **beaches of Guincho** and the **Cabo da Roca**, situated some six miles away. On this side of town, you will also find the **Palácio dos Condes de Castro Guimarães**: a library and museum. In the grounds, visit the **Chapel of São Sebastião** and its 17th-century polychrome *azulejos*. Further to the west of the town is the **Praça dos touros**, the largest bullring in Portugal which now hosts few bullfights due to its exposed position.

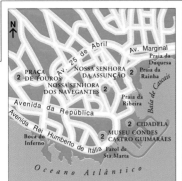

From Cascais, you can go on foot to the Boca do Inferno (Mouth of Hell), where you can gaze down into a roaring gorge.

Sintra is one of the most interesting towns around Lisbon, for its artistic, historical, and natural riches as well as its outstanding old quarters (*Vila Vehla*) that have hardly changed in two centuries. On your way, before entering the Sintra mountain range, stop at the Palace of Queluz, the most visited and most famous royal residence in Portugal.

Further afield

Queluz (3)

Known as the 'little Versailles,' the **Palace of Queluz** is a fine example of late 18th-century baroque architecture, surrounded by lush vegetation. Originally the country residence of the Marquês de Castelo Rodrigo in the 17th century, it became the summer palace of the Portuguese royal family during the reign of João V (1706–50) and later the royal residence of Maria I (1777–1816). The palace is a clever mixture of baroque and neoclassical styles, designed by the architects Mateus Vicente de Oliveira and the Frenchman Jean-Baptiste Robillon. The interior decoration is particularly stunning with its crystal chandeliers, gilded woodcarvings, and mirrors. Of particular note are the Throne Room, where concerts are held during the Sintra Classical Music Festival, the Don Quixote Room, a former royal bedroom that owes its name to the paintings of Cervantes' hero that line the walls and circular ceiling, as well as the Lion Staircase, and the famous Robillon Lodge. Outside, enjoy a walk in one of the many gardens, including the large Canal garden and the Neptune garden in front of the rococo-style ceremonial façade, both filled with sculptures, benches covered with *azulejos,* and fountains. The Neptune fountain is by Bernini.

Sintra (4)

This area of outstanding natural beauty has been listed by UNESCO as one of the world's natural treasures. It has one of the most interesting examples of Romantic architecture in the world. Dominating Sintra is the **Palácio Nacional**, crowned by the two chimneys that have become the symbol of the town. It is unique in that it is the only royal residence in Portugal that has survived from the Middle Ages, even though it has undergone many modifications. Originally a Moorish palace in the 11th century, it was rebuilt by João I and Manuel I in the 15th and 16th centuries. Of particular interest are the so-called Manueline Wing in the east, the Swan Room in the center, the Mecca Courtyard and Gothic chapel in the north, and the Shield Room in the west that houses the largest collection of Mudéjar *azulejos* in the world (15th and 16th centuries). Also of note are the hanging gardens and the breathtaking view over the mountain range. Other places of interest in the area include the **house/museum of the writer Ferreira de Castro** containing some of his personal possessions and paintings by Cândido Portinari and Júlio Pomar, and the **Igreja de São Martinho** with its attractive altar screen by Diogo de Contreiras. If you continue along the steep narrow path (*trilha*), you will eventually reach the **Castelo dos Mouros** at the top of the hill, a structure that was carved into the rock face by the Moors and predates the Christian invasion of 1147. Finally, in the heart of the **Pena Park** stands the **Pena Palace**. Built between 1838 and 1840 by Ferdinand II of Saxe-Coburg-Gotha on the site of a ruined monastery, this palace was the last residence of Manuel II before his exile in 1910. The Romantic building, by the architects Possidónio da Silva and Baron von Eschwege, is a fine example of neo-medieval revival, predating by some 20 years the castles of Ludwig of Bavaria. The stuccos, frescos, furniture, and paintings all provide an excellent account of life in the castle during the 19th century. Of the former monastery, you can still visit the cloisters and a beautiful chapel containing a marble altar screen by the sculptor Nicolas de Chantereine (1532). Visit too the **Colecção Bérardo** with its 400 late 20th-century works of art, which were all collected by the businessman José Bérnardo.

This route follows the ridge of the Serra de Arrábida. Hidden among the oaks and pines of this nature reserve are a number of retreats and chapels built in the 16th century, as well as panoramic viewing platforms with stunning views over the area. Far below, the ocher cliffs plunge down to the turquoise sea where fishing boats weave in and out.

Further afield

Costa da Caparica (5) and Cabo Espichel (6)

The Costa da Caparica is a series of large beaches dominated by ocher-red dunes and scattered with quaint little bars. As soon as the weather turns warmer, the place becomes a magnet for bathers and surfers. At the very end of the promontory, the **Sanctuary of Nossa Senhora do Cabo** was built to commemorate a vision of the Virgin in the 15th century. Until the 18th century, the church was quite small but today's sanctuary (1707) is an example of the style of architecture engendered by pilgrimages, complete with aqueduct, and two strange long wings that surround the church and that were used for accommodating pilgrims. The church (built by João Antunes) is worth a visit for its baroque painting by Lourenço Cunha (1740) on the ceiling (somewhat damaged), its choir, with a gallery dating from the 18th century, and paintings of Santo Tiago and Santo António from the original church.

Sesimbra (7)

In Santana follow the winding road round to Sesimbra, a fishing center specializing in swordfish and situated in a natural amphitheater. The town is dominated by the **castle** which fell into the hands of Afonso I in 1165 and was then destroyed in 1191 by the Moors who had originally built it. Rebuilding work was begun by Denis I and continued by João IV in the 17th century. The fortress, now tastefully restored, has magnificent views over a large part of the coast and, to the southeast, over the **Serra da Arrábida**. The **Igreja de Nossa Senhora da Consolação** is within the fortress walls. In the town, visit the **Igreja de São Tiago** and the **Igreja da Misericórdia** with a painting on wood attributed to Gregório Lopes (1535). Built on the beach, the **Fortress of São Tiago** is a wonderful example of 17th-century defensive architecture.

Vila Fresca de Azeitão (8) and Quinta de Bacalhoa (9)

On the road to Lisbon, visit the **Vila Fresca de Azeitão**, at the foot of the Arrábida mountain range. The **Igreja de São Lourenço** contains an Italian Renaissance-style Virgin and Child from the studio of Della Robbia. Also dating from the Renaissance is the fountain that stands at the side of the road, decorated with a bas-relief depicting prophets and sibyls. During the Renaissance, the town was visited by well-off members of a bourgeoisie that were very interested in art. ★ At the Saturday morning market you can buy the famous azeitão cheese ➡ 132. Not far away is one of the oldest manor houses still inhabited in Portugal, the **Quintas de Bacalhoa**, built in 1480 and restored in the 20th century. This private property is often opened to the public, but visiting times are short. Of interest are the archways, gardens, ponds and small Italian temples.

Setúbal (10)

Visit Setúbal to the east, one of Portugal's oldest cities and now heavily industrialized. Its showpiece is the **Igreja do Jesus**, built in 1491, with an interior decorated by Boytac (one of the master architects of the Belém Monastery). The cabled columns supporting the nave are particularly distinctive. The adjoining cloisters house a collection of Portuguese primitives from the 15th and 16th centuries. The town's other attractions include the **Castelo de São Filipe**, **Praça do Bocage**, with its statue of the poet born in the town, and the **Regional Museum of Archeology and Ethnography**, containing many Roman remains. Early in the morning at the port, see the fishing boats return, the colorful trawlers unload their catches, and fishermen repair their nets. Sail to the Tróia Peninsula, a large inland sea with vast salt marshes.

Estremadura is a treasure trove of things to see and visit. Those interested in architecture will be seduced by one of the most complete panoramas of Portuguese styles in the country. To the north stand the monasteries of Batalha and Alcobaça and, not far from Lisbon, a large number of royal residences built over the centuries, such as the one at Mafra. Small towns,

Further afield

Mafra (11)

The journey to Mafra is short but tortuous. The road follows the contours of the landscape, rising, falling, and twisting around mountains and valleys. As you approach the Royal Palace of Mafra, it is easy to imagine the difficulties that must have been encountered when building in such a location. The **Palácio-Convento de Mafra** was the ambitious project of Dom João V, the Magnanimous, built between 1713 and 1730 by the German architect J. F. Ludwig. The overall architectural style of the monument seeks to convey the stability of absolutism, combining a royal residence with monastic and secular institutions (represented by the monastery and the basilica). The most striking illustration of this aim is the symmetry of the two palaces, that of the king and that of the queen, in relation to the central church. At each corner, the palace is crowned with stark towers that have a military air about them. This grandiloquent architectural project was made possible by the Brazilian gold from Minas Gerais, a discovery that also explains the baroque luxury of the sculptures, paintings, and Italian marble statues and the prestigious collection of works in the famous library. In the town itself, visit the **Igreja de Santo André**, a beautiful 14th-century Gothic building and once the church of Pedro Hispano who became Pope John XXI.

Ericeira (12)

Not far from Mafra, the picturesque fishing village of Ericeira on the Estremadura coast was founded by royal privilege in 1229. Blending perfectly into the steep coastline, it is noted for its three beaches bordering the rough sea and its maze of streets, squares, and quaint alleyways. Its many fish and seafood restaurants are also of great repute. It is from here that the Portuguese royal family fled in exile to England following the victory of the Republican movement on October 5, 1910. In the historical center of the town, a number of monuments deserve particular attention. The **chapels of Santo António** and **São Sebastião** contain polychrome *azulejos* dating from the 17th century and the main church dedicated to **São Pedro** boasts rococo *talhas* (gilded woodcarvings), and canvases by Manuel António de Góis (1760). The collections of thanksgiving plaques on the theme of the sea and procession banners in the **Igreja da Misericórdia** are also well worth looking at.

Colares (13)

On your way back from Ericeira, pass by the beautiful beaches of Azenhas do Mar and Maçãs and stop off at Colares. Founded in 1561 by royal privilege of Manuel I, this last northern bastion of the area protected by Sintra and Cascais is certainly one of the most charming towns around. It is from this period that the magnificent Manueline pillory dates, standing as it does on the square where once the buildings of the former local government were to be found. Not far from here is the **Igreja da Misericórdia**, containing a mannerist altar screen painted by Cristóvão Vaz, and the Renaissance **Igreja da Assunção**, in which the walls are covered with 17th-century *azulejos*. In the main chapel, the baroque marble altar screen by the architect João Antunes (1701) and the blue and white *azulejos* by the painter António Pereira (in particular the *Flight to Egypt* from around 1710) are worth seeing.

landscapes, beaches, and fishing ports all invite the visitor to explore further.

Where to shop

Sales

The stores in Lisbon hold sales twice a year: from January 15 to February 15; and from August 15 to September 15.

Leather goods

If you're looking for a bargain, check out the leather goods, particularly shoes and bags. Top quality goods at unbeatable prices.

Opening times

Most stores and businesses open from Monday to Friday (9am–1pm, 3–7pm). In theory, they are closed on Saturday afternoon, Sunday and public holidays but more and more stores are now opening during lunch and on Saturday afternoon.

43 Shops

THE INSIDER'S FAVORITES

What to take home?

A bottle of port ➙ 132, 134, 136, 146, a *presunto* (smoked ham) ➙ 132, 146, a can of sardines ➙ 132, *marmelada* (quince jam) or a selection of fresh cakes ➙ 132, 144; a panel of *azulejos*, a ceramic vase, hand-embroidered cotton or linen, an Arraiolos rug, a leather bag and shoes ➙ 136, 138, 140, 146, 147; or maybe, as the pièce de résistance, a recording of *fados* ➙ 134 and a book of Pessoa's texts ➙ 134, 140

The opening of the Amoreiras Shopping Center in 1985 marked the beginning of the modernization of shopping centers in Lisbon and a decisive change in shopping habits. Another new complex is going up in the north of the city, an area bristling with post-modernist towers, occupied by advertising agencies, banks and communication companies.

Where to shop

Amoreiras Shopping Center (1)
Av. Eng. Duarte Pacheco, 1070 ☎ 381 02 40 ➡ 383 27 35

Ⓜ *Rotunda* 🚊 *11, 48, 58* 🕐 *daily 9am–midnight; closed Christmas, New Year*
▣ 🍴 ▼ 🖪 ⛷ ✂

This imposing futuristic complex is the work of Tomás Taveira, who is one of Lisbon's most prominent architects. There was much public outcry against the construction of this huge shopping center which is right in the middle of the city. The Amoreiras contains 300 stores, 55 restaurants, pizzerias, and fast-food outlets, 10 movie theaters, a bingo hall, numerous banks, a post office, a health club with a swimming pool, tennis courts, supermarket, several beauty salons and even a Roman Catholic chapel! ★ This is an ideal place for shopping on Saturday afternoons or on Sundays when nearly all the other stores in the city are closed.

Centro Comercial Colombo (2)
Av. Lusíada, 1500 ☎ 716 02 50

Ⓜ *Colégio Militar* 🚊 *50, 65, 69, 85* 🕐 *daily 10am–midnight* ▣ 🍴 ▼ 🖪

Colombo is Lisbon's newest shopping center; it was opened in September 1997 in the northwest of the city. It seems to have overtaken the Amoreiras in popularity and claims to be the biggest shopping center in Europe. However, opinions remain divided on this point as well as on its esthetic merits. There is a wide range of different stores within the complex selling furniture, perfumery, interior design and books. It also houses Lisbon's largest Habitat store as well as movie theaters and a variety of restaurants.

Printemps (3)
28, rua do Carmo, edifício Grandela, 1200
☎ 321 98 00 ➡ 321 98 43

Ⓜ *Rossio, Chiado* 🚊 *tram 28* 🕐 *Mon.–Sat. 10am–8pm* ▣ *tax-free*

Printemps is housed in the Grandela building, and was built at the turn of the century in the style of the large Parisian department store of the same name. Destroyed in a fire in 1988, it has recently been rebuilt by the architect Álvaro Siza Vieira ➡ 88. The five-storey stocks a large range of products: cosmetics, perfume, ready-to-wear fashion, houseware and sports equipment.

Galerias Monumental (4)
51, av. Fontes Pereira de Melo, 1050 ☎ 315 05 31 ➡ 315 05 37

Ⓜ *Saldanha* 🕐 *open daily 10am–12pm; closed Christmas, New Year* ▣ *tax-free*
🍴 ▼ 🖪

This shopping center is smaller than the others but still has room for four movie theaters, a restaurant and several fast-food outlets. The Coronel Tapioca is worth visiting for its vast range of camping equipment and its high-quality travel goods.

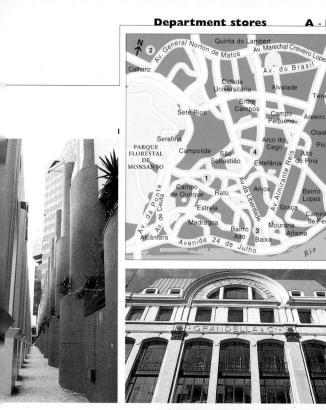

The Amoreiras Shopping Center, with its imposing chrome façade, dominates the center of Lisbon.

In the area

Jewelers, watchmakers and stores selling metalware still abound in the Rua da Prata and the Rua do Ouro. The Baixa has always been Lisbon's commercial center. Its busy cobbled streets are also home to a number of hotels and businesses. ■ Where to stay ➡ 19 ➡ 20 ■ Where to

Where to shop

Manuel Tavares (5)
1-AB, rua da Betesga, 1100 ☎ 342 42 09

Ⓜ *Rossio* 🔆 *tram 15* **Cooked meats, cheese, wine** Ⓢ *Mon.–Sat. 9.30am–7.30pm* ▣

An old, well-established delicatessen selling a wide variety of typical Portuguese products: *enchidos* (sausages), an essential ingredient for the traditional dish, *cozido à portuguesa* (a kind of stew), *salpicão* (garlic sausage), *morcelas da Guarda* (sausage flavored with onion, parsley and wine), *chorizo* from the Alentejo, *preseunto serrano* (ham). There is a good choice of sheep's cheese: *amenteigado* from the Serra da Estrela (a soft cheese which is often eaten spread on bread with quince jam) and *azeitão* ➡ 124 (another soft cheese). It also sells homemade compotes, locally produced bread, honey cake (a Madeiran specialty), and a good range of wines.

Confeitaria Nacional (6)
18-B, praça da Figueira, 1100 ☎ 342 44 70

Ⓜ *Rossio* **Cakes and pastries** Ⓢ *Mon.–Fri. 8am–8.30pm, Sat. 8am–2pm* ▤ 🏨

Copper decoration and soft lighting contribute to the chic and elegant atmosphere of the Confeitaria Nacional, a well-known patisserie and café. Local people come here to buy the *bolo rei* (a traditional Portuguese cake made with dried fruit and sugar) at Christmas and Easter time. Other traditional Portuguese cakes on sale are *queijadas de Sintra* (cheese cakes), *bolas de Berlim* (cream doughnuts), *doces de ovos de Aveiro*, éclairs and mille-feuilles. All these delicious pastries and cakes are made with large quantities of eggs and sugar and are full of calories. ★ Lunch is served here too.

Conserveira de Lisboa (7)
34, rua dos Bacalhoeiros, 1100 ☎ 887 10 58

🔆 *37, tram 28* **Bottled preserves and cans** Ⓢ *Mon.–Fri. 9am–1.30pm, 2.30–7pm; Sat. 9am–1.30pm* ▤

This store is full of row upon row of preserves and cans that have been arranged and labeled with great care. Tuna, sardines and anchovies are the most common ingredients in Portuguese cooking and these are on sale here preserved and canned in every way imaginable. As is the custom in most Portuguese stores, each purchase is carefully wrapped up in white paper.

Not forgetting

■ **Casa Macário (8)** 272–276, rua Augusta, 1100 ☎ 342 09 00 ➡ 342 90 29 *Port, compotes, sweetmeats, dried fruit, tea and imported chocolate. Coffee-tasting.*
■ **Pastelaria Suíça (9)** 100, praça Dom Pedro IV, 1100 ☎ 342 80 92 or 342 80 93 ➡ 346 47 88 *A patisserie, that is located on a very busy square, selling a range of excellent cakes and pastries at more affordable prices than at the Confeiteria Nacional. The terrace is a very popular place for breakfast.*

eat ➡ 34 ➡ 35 ➡ 36 ➡ 38
■ After dark ➡ 76 ■ What
to see ➡ 86 ➡ 92 ■ Where
to shop ➡ 134

In the patisseries of Lisbon,
you can choose any cake
you desire and eat it
there as well.

In the area
With its fine baroque churches and elegant boutiques, a stroll in
the Chiado, now restored by Álvaro Siza Vieira after the fire of 1988,
is always a pleasure. ■ Where to stay ➡ 20 ■ Where to eat ➡ 38
➡ 41 ■ After dark ➡ 64 ➡ 65 ➡ 66 ■ What to see ➡ 84 ➡ 86 ➡ 88

➡ Where to shop

Casa Pereira (10)
38, rua Garrett, 1200 ☎ 342 66 94

Ⓜ *Chiado, tram 15* **Wine, liqueurs, delicatessen** Ⓢ *Mon.–Fri. 9.30am–7.30 pm;
Sat. 9am–1pm* ▭

The Casa Pereira has all the charm of a typical Portuguese delicatessen: a
hundred and one products are artistically arranged on attractive shelves.
There is a wide variety of coffee (ground or in beans, and sold by the
kilo), chocolate and tea. You can also buy traditional wines and liqueurs,
such as the Moscatel de Setúbal ➡ 124, Serrano liqueur and *aguardente
de Zimbro* (brandy). ★ Other recommended specialties are the ice cream,
the compotes and especially the *rosmaninho* (rosemary honey) with nuts.
There is also a very good selection of cakes.

Virgin (11)
17, praça dos Restauradores, antigo edifício Eden, 1250
☎ 346 03 09 ➡ 346 03 53

Ⓜ *Restauradores* **CDs, cassettes, videos, hi-fi accessories** Ⓢ *Mon.–Sat.
10am–9.45pm; Sun. 2–7.45pm* ▭ ▭ *tax-free*

Spread over three floors, Lisbon's Virgin Megastore sells all kinds of music
on CD and cassette as well as specialist magazines, video cassettes and
personal stereos. There is a book section, but no proper bookstore.
There is no ticket sales outlet either.

Celeiro Dieta (12)
65, rua 1° de Dezembro, 1200 ☎ 342 70 51 ➡ 347 22 69

Ⓜ *Chiado, tram 15* **Vegetarian and macrobiotic products** Ⓢ *Mon.–Sat.
8.30am–7.30pm* ▭ ⓘ ⓘ *85-A, avenida da República* ☎ *795 28 23;
43-B, rua Coelho da Rocha* ☎ *397 16 48*

A supermarket specializing in vegetarian and macrobiotic products.
Tea and a variety of homeopathic medicines are also stocked. This is
one of the few places in Lisbon where you can find Asian products
such as *seitan* and *tofu*. There is also a wide range of books on the
subject and a macrobiotic restaurant in the basement, which gets
fairly busy at lunch time.

Not forgetting

■ **Ourivesaria Sarmento (13)** 251, rua Áurea, 1100 ☎ 342 67 74
➡ 347 07 83 *A traditional Lisbon jeweler's founded in 1870. Good quality filigree
jewelry, exquisite pieces and silverware.*
■ **Férin (14)** 72, rua Nova do Almada, 1200 ☎ 342 44 22 ➡ 347 11 01
*This is one of the most traditional bookshops in Lisbon. Thousands of books line
the beautiful dark wood shelves. It specializes in French literature and essays, in
law, art and books about economics.*
■ **Livraria Bertrand (15)** 73, rua Garrett, 1200 ☎ 346 86 46
➡ 342 42 75 *This large bookstore, which is located in the heart of the Chiado,
is easily recognizable by its splendid façade which is decorated with blue and
white azulejos. It houses a good range of books including a wide selection of
travel books.*

■ Where to shop ➡ 142

LISBOA

The commercial area of Chiado is a paradise of small stores, art galleries and book stores.

A stroll down the lively rua do Alecrim, with its numerous antique stores, is always pleasant. Start from Cais do Sodré and climb up to the Bairro Alto until you reach the Miradouro São Pedro ➡ 84 where you'll get splendid views over the Tagus. ■ Where to stay ➡ 20 ■ Where to eat

Where to shop

Leitão & Irmão
Antigos Joalheiros da Coroa (16)
8, travessa da Espera, 1200 ☎ 342 41 07 ➡ 342 95 53

🔲 58, 100, tram 28 **Jewelry** 🕐 Mon.–Fri. 10am–1pm, 2–7pm 🔲

Leitão & Irmão is the oldest and most distinguished jeweler in the city of Lisbon. Established two hundred years ago, it is still thought of as the official jeweler to the crown, despite the fact that the monarchy was overthrown long ago. Customers are welcomed into a splendid waiting room which is furnished with comfortable sofas. Most of the pieces are made of gold but silver and precious stones are also used. ★ Commissions are undertaken and carried out by in-house engravers and jewelers.

Solar do Vinho do Porto (17)
45, rua de São Pedro de Alcântara, 1250
☎ 347 57 07 ➡ 347 83 92

🔲 58, 100 **Wines** 🕐 Mon.–Fri. 10am–11.45pm, Sat. 11am–10.45pm; closed holidays 🔲 🔶 Outlet at Portela airport

The aim of this establishment is to introduce its customers to the many varieties of port wine that are produced in Portugal. In a darkened room with a dimly lit bar you are able to taste more than 300 different port wines. If you are very persuasive you might be able to take a free bottle or two away with you. ★ This is an ideal place to try out different wines before going out to buy them in larger quantities in specialist stores.

Ourivesaria Silva (18)
40, praça Luís de Camões, 1200
☎ 342 27 28 or 342 63 20 ➡ 342 63 69

🔲 58, 100 **Silverware** 🕐 Mon.–Fri. 10am–1pm, 3–7pm; Sat. 9am–1pm 🔲 tax-free

Ourivesaria Silva specializes in 16th-, 17th- and 18th-century silverware. It sells jewels, brooches, precious stones as well as reproductions of antique jewelry and some second-hand pieces. A workshop which is attached to the store carries out repairs and also restoration on antique jewelry.

Not forgetting

■ **Casa Regional da Ilha Verde (19)** 4, rua Paiva de Andrade, 1200 ☎ 342 59 74 *Beautiful examples of Portuguese artistry. The handicrafts to be found here include embroidery from the Açores, and hand-embroidered linen cloths tablecloths, sheets and bathroom and kitchen towels.*
■ **Loja da Atalaia (20)** 71, rua da Atalaia, 1200 ☎ 346 20 93 ➡ 342 15 65 *A wonderful store in the heart of the Bairro Alto, which sells designer items and furniture. The articles are so well displayed you would think you were walking around an exhibition. Contemporary, modern Portuguese design as well as some traditional lines.*

17

20

8

Multicolored Moorish motifs and blue and white tiles adorn the façades of numerous houses, from the humblest dwellings to the most sumptuous palaces. Azulejos, which provide very effective protection against fire, started to be imported into Lisbon in the 15th century and became especially commonplace after the earthquake in 1755. Museu do Azulejo ➥ 96.

Where to shop

Vista Alegre (21)
18, largo do Chiado, 1200 ☎ 346 14 01 ➥ 347 01 68

⊞ 58, 100, tram 28 **Porcelain, glassware, earthenware** ◐ Mon.–Sat. 9.30am–7pm ☐ tax-free ⬥ numerous ☎ 346 14 01

Vista Alegre, located in the heart of the Chiado, has been in business since 1829 and sells its own range of fine porcelain as well as glassware, crystal and earthenware. Young Portuguese couples often leave their wedding lists here. Until 1989, few people had access to Vista Alegre's products because you could only buy a complete dinner service. But since this time the store has relaxed its rules and as a result now allows customers to buy individual pieces, which has led to it becoming much more popular. It has also started to diversify its stock and now also sells tablecloths, houseware, salt and pepper shakers, kitchen accessories and glassware. The designs range from the really traditional to the very modern.

Depósito da Marinha Grande (22)
234, rua de São Bento, 1200 ☎ 396 32 34 ➥ 396 56 93

Ⓜ Rato ⊞ 10, tram 25, 28 **Glasses and crystal** ◐ Mon.–Fri. 9am–1pm, 3–7pm; Sat. 9am–1pm ☐ tax-free ⬥ Centro Comercial Colombo ➥ 130 ☎ 716 31 20

Hidden away behind a magnificent blue and white façade of *azulejos* is the Marinha Grande warehouse. Marinha Grande crystal is considered to be the best in Portugal. The shelves are piled high with glass and crystal which are all on sale at factory prices. ★ Some pieces are flawed or may be factory seconds, but if you look carefully enough you can unearth some real treasures. At the store down the road (no. 420) you can find the same products, in perfect condition but at much higher prices.

Fábrica Sant'Anna (23)
93–95, rua do Alecrim, 1200 ☎ 342 25 37 ➥ 347 67 46

Ⓜ Rato ⊞ 58, 100, tram 28 **Azulejos** ◐ Mon.–Fri. 9.30am–7pm; Sat. 10am–2pm ☐ tax-free

As well as a wide range of *azulejos* with traditional designs, this factory-store also stocks vases, light fittings, gardening equipment, plates and various other decorative articles all displayed in a very higgledy-piggledy fashion. The Fabrica was founded in 1741 and continues to employ 18th-century manufacturing techniques. ★ Customers can also visit the factory and purchase items there.

Not forgetting
■ **Ratton Cerâmicas (24)** 2-C, rua da Academia das Ciências, 1200 ☎ 346 09 48 *This gallery both exhibits and sells azulejos designed by contemporary artists such as Paula Rego, Graça Morais, Júlio Pomar, Lurdes de Castro, Menez, Pedro Proença, Jorge Martins, Costa Pinheiros, Stock Lein, Bartolomeu Cid and João Vieira.*

24

18 VA 24
VISTA ALEGRE

22

FÁBRICA SANT'ANNA
FUNDADA EM 1741
CERAMICA ARTISTICA

23

21

The Rato district gets its name from a Mr. Ratton, a French industrialist who fled the French Revolution and set up china factories and weaving industries in the area. ■ Where to stay ➡ 18 ➡ 22 ➡ 24 ■ Where to eat ➡ 44 ➡ 48 ■ After dark ➡ 68 ➡ 72 ➡ 74 ➡ 76 ➡ 78

➡ **Where to shop**

Tourist House (25)
159, avenida da Liberdade, 1250 ☎ 315 15 58 ➡ 353 83 00

Ⓜ *Avenida da Liberdade* **Portuguese crafts** 🕐 *Mon.–Fri. 9am–1pm, 3–7pm. Sat. 9am–1pm, 4–7pm; Sun. 10am–noon* 🔲 *tax-free* 🏧 *rua Augusta*

The numerous craft stores that are scattered about Lisbon are only rarely frequented by the Portuguese. The Tourist House demonstrates why this may be through its prominent line of T-shirts emblazoned with internationally familiar witticisms such as "Portuguese do it better." Not all its wares are of such limited appeal, however, and it also stocks china and ceramics from Coïmbra, Agathe, Malveira and Alentejo; woolen sweaters from Povoa, called *poveiras*; tablecloths, scarves and tablemats from Madeira, Vianan do Castelo and Lixa; dolls in national costume. In short, a really wide range of Portuguese regional crafts.

Casa dos Tapetes de Arraiolos (26)
116-E, rua da Imprensa Nacional, 1250 ☎ 396 33 54 ➡ 395 00 63

Ⓜ *Rotunda* 🔳 *58* **Rugs** 🕐 *Mon.–Fri. 9.30am–1pm, 3–7pm; Sat. 9.30am–1pm* 🔲 *tax-free* 🏧 *rua Augusta*

Arraiolos, which are traditional Portuguese rugs, are renowned for the outstanding beauty of their designs. Made entirely by hand, they are then also hand-decorated with pure wool embroidery. When buying one, be sure to look carefully at the quality of both the materials and the workmanship. A rug made with pure wool and high quality base fabric can be expected to remain in good condition for about 30 years.

Buchholz (27)
4, rua Duque de Palmela, 1200 ☎ 317 05 80 ➡ 352 26 34

Ⓜ *Rotunda* **Books** 🕐 *Mon.–Fri. 9am–6pm; Sat. 9am–1pm* 🔲

Behind an unassuming façade nestles a delightful bookstore which is rated as one of the best in Lisbon. As well as stocking Portuguese books, the shop also has a good foreign literature section (mainly English, French and German). There is also a good selection of classical and New Age audio CDs. ★ Buy a coffee at the bookstore's in-house bar and spend a peaceful hour or two dipping into some of the titles on display, which are almost certain to include one or two of your favorites.

Galeria Luís Serpa (28)
1-B, rua Tenente Raúl Cascais, 1250 ☎ 397 77 44 ➡ 397 02 51

Ⓜ *Rato* 🔳 *58* **Art gallery** 🕐 *Mon.–Sat. 2.30–7.30pm; closed during public holidays* 🔲

The Galeria Luís Serpa introduced the Portuguese to post-modernism. It has displays of sculpture, paintings and photographs by famous Portuguese artists, such as Sarmento, Pedro Cabrita Reis, Jorge Molder, Rui Sanches and Daniel Blaufuks, as well as international ones. All the art on display in the gallery is for sale.

What to see
➡ 102 ➡ 110
Where to
shop ➡ 142

27

25

Azulejos of every
size, color and
motif are on
sale. Pick your
own and make
a fresco!

25

The *Moda Lisboa* fashion show which takes place twice a year in Lisbon is proof that Portuguese fashion design is alive and flourishing. The show, set up nine years ago by Eduardo Abbondarie and Mário Matas Ribeiro with the backing of the mayor of Lisbon, is a showcase for Portuguese talent. Ana Salazar was one of the first designers to enjoy international renown,

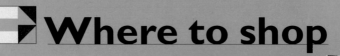

Where to shop

José António Tenente (29)

8, travessa do Carmo, 1200
☎ 342 25 60
⇒ 347 73 18
Ready-to-wear fashion
◉ Mon.–Sat. 10.30am–7.30pm
▭

An architect before entering the world of fashion, António Tenente won the Expo '98 competition. His store, which opened in 1990, stocks his collections for men and women. He has built up a strong following and his fashion collections are regularly shown at the *Moda Lisboa*.

Ana Salazar (30)

87, rua do Carmo, 1200
☎ 347 22 89
Ready-to-wear fashion
◉ Mon.–Sat. 10am–7pm ▭

Ana Salazar is one of Portugal's most widely known fashion designers whose work has earned international acclaim. Her ready-to-wear collections are sold in Paris, Tokyo, Milan and New York. She has also brought out a line of fashions for men, together with a range of fashion accessories including glasses, wallets, shoes, belts, jewelry and perfume.

José Carlos (31)

2, travessa do Monte do Carmo, 1250
☎ 321 95 80
⇒ 321 95 89
Designer fashion
▣ 100
◉ Mon.–Fri. 11am–8pm; Sat. 11am–3pm

Fashion designer José Carlos first started work as a hair stylist before opening his own design workshop and then showing his own fashion collections from time to time. His store is located in the center of the Principe Real district and his stylish clothes are worn by a large section of Portuguese high society.

Manuel Alves & José Manuel Gonçalves (31)

85–87, rua da Rosa, 1200
☎ 342 25 09
⇒ 347 51 37
Ready-to-wear fashion
Ⓜ Chiado ◉
Mon.–Fri. 11am–1pm, 2–8pm; Sat. 11am–1pm, 2–4pm

Design gurus, Alves & Gonçalves, create fashion for both men and women. Their designs are especially popular with media personalities and the Portuguese jet set. At their store, you might even be greeted by the designers themselves.

followed by Fátima Lopes, José António Tenente and Manuel Alves & José Manuel Gonçalves.

Lena Aires (33)

96, rua da Atalaia, 1200

☎ 346 18 15

➠ 342 83 46

Ready-to-wear fashion for women

▣ tram 28

◷ Mon.–Fri. 12.30–8pm, Sat. 3–8pm ▭

Lena Aires was the first Portuguese fashion designer to be featured in *Vogue* magazine. She started her career by showing her creations at small-scale fashion events and has recently stirred up a lot of interest at the *Moda Lisboa*. Her designs for clothes are very daring and bold.

Fátima Lopes (34)

44-E, avenida de Roma, 1700

☎ 849 59 86

➠ 796 62 28

Ready-to-wear fashion ▣ 7, 37

◷ Mon.–Sat. 10.30am–7.30pm

▭

Fatima Lopes comes from the island of Madeira. She received no formal training in design. Her first sensuous, sexy collection was shown in 1992 in the Beato monastery. her rise in popularity has been rapid. She now exports her collections all over Europe, the United States and Asia. She opened her first boutique in Paris in 1996.

Gardénia Young Fashion (35)

96, rua Nova do Almada, 1200

☎ 347 20 26

➠ 346 39 55

Street fashion

▣ tram 28

◷ Mon.–Sat. 10am–8pm ▭

Gardénia Young Fashion stocks ready-to-wear from most of the top international fashion names as well as popular Portuguese designer labels such as Nuno Gama and Luís Buchinho. Unisex fashion and menswear are spread over three floors. ★ The store specializes in expensive clothes for the young and trendy.

Iznougud (36)

113, avenida Almirante Reis, CC Portugália, 1150

☎ 352 35 92

➠ 357 07 04

Street fashion

▣ 7, 8, 40, tram 28

◷ Mon.–Fri. 10.30am–2pm, 3–8pm; Sat. 11am–2pm, 3–7pm ▣

This store is well worth a visit if only to admire the really unusual decor. It stocks fashions by young Portuguese designers as well as London imports. ★ In the sportswear section there is a collection of second-hand Adidas tracksuits which date back to the 1970s.

The opening of the Centro Cultural de Belém ➡ 78 ➡ 104 has significantly livened up the area. Its numerous specialist stores, galleries and green spaces draw many visitors. ■ Where to eat ➡ 54 ■ After dark ➡ 78 ■ What to see ➡ 104 ➡ 106 ➡ 110

➡ Where to shop

37

Confeitaria de Belém (37)
84–92, rua de Belém, 1300 ☎ 363 74 23 ➡ 363 80 77 or 363 80 78

🚌 27, 49, tram 15 **Pastries and cakes** 🕐 *open daily 8am–midnight* 🚭 ♿

A visit to Belém wouldn't be complete without calling in at its famous *confeitaria*: a charming, traditional patisserie at one of Lisbon's smartest addresses. This famous house which is over a hundred years old is located in a very pretty street and its ancient façade is decorated with *azulejos* in a variety of different designs and motifs. The Confeitaria is actually both a bakery and a tea-shop, and inside it is decorated with blue and white ceramics. Since 1837 the Confeitaria has produced its own *pasteis de Belém* made according to a traditional recipe from Mosteiro dos Jeronimos. These are delicious little custard tarts which are served hot – straight out of the oven – and placed facing each other so that the filling does not get cold. They are often served sprinkled with icing sugar and cinnamon. The Confeitaria also makes other delicious little cakes and mille-feuilles. It is a favorite meeting place and so is often very crowded with both local people and visitors to the city – do not be surprised if you have to wait a while before finding a table to sit down. ★ Alternatively, you can always buy a dozen *pastéis* and have them wrapped up in attractive little boxes (sachets of sugar and cinnamon included!) and take them out to savor them while sitting on a seat by the riverfront – for example in the charming Jardim do Ultramar ➡ 110 – or while walking along the road to the Mosteiro dos Jerónimos ➡ 106, which is just a stone's throw away.

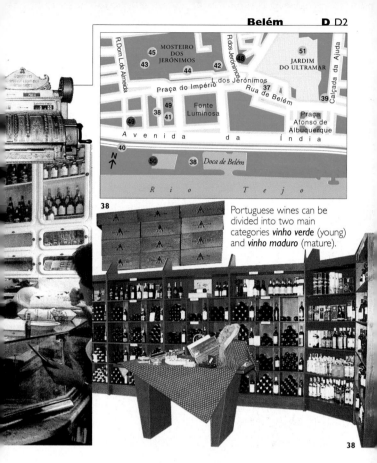

38

Portuguese wines can be divided into two main categories *vinho verde* (young) and *vinho maduro* (mature).

38

Coisas do Arco do Vinho (38)
Centro Cultural de Belém, rua Bartolomeu Dias, loja 7, 1300
☎ 364 20 31 or 364 20 32 ➡ 364 20 31

🚌 29, 43, tram 15 **Wines** 🕐 Tue.–Sun. 2–8pm 📦 delivery overseas 💳

The Coisas do Arco do Vinho, which is located on the first floor of the Centro Cultural de Belém just by the Portuguese Film Institute, is considered to be the best wineseller in Lisbon. It is also the only shop of its kind in the whole of Portugal, in its wise decision to sell not only fine wines but also the best things to accompany wine, from drinking accessories to mouth-watering food specialties. Naturally, it stocks the best port wines, especially those of 1994, which experts reckon to be the finest vintage of the century. They also have the best regional wines (red and white) and numerous fascinating accessories for wine drinkers – corkscrews, Riedel glasses, stoppers, carafes. . . In addition there is a delicatessen (foie gras, caviar, pheasant pâté, preserves, olive oil, special vinegars and fruit preserves) as well as a selection of books on wine. All their products are reasonably priced. The two managers, Francisco Barâo da Cunha and José Oliveira Azevedo, are wine specialists and will be only too pleased to give advice. ★ It aims to be a cultural center and as a result not only hosts regular wine-tasting events but also book launches and exhibitions of art related to wine. Expo '98 will be an occasion for many different events organized in collaboration with the Centro Cultural de Belém ➡ 78 ➡ 104. Lovers of good wine and great food will certainly not be disappointed.

There are many pleasant walks in Lisbon. One suggested route involves a stroll around the Alfama near the São Vicente and Campo Santa Clara where numerous antique dealers have set up business. Further down, near the Tagus, in Rua de São Pedro, a picturesque fish market takes place every morning. To the west of the Baixa you can climb back up the hill along Rua

Where to shop

40

Lisbon has a number of markets that are held every day somewhere in the capital. Here you can buy fresh produce from the country areas, along with many regional specialties.

40

Feira da Ladra (39)

Campo de Santa Clara
🚋 tram 28
🕐 winter: Tue., Sat. 6am–2pm/ summer: Tues., Sat. 6am–4pm 🏧

This flea market has become something of an institution in Lisbon. It takes place in all weathers, rain or shine. You'll find a lot of old-fashioned junk, as well as new

and second-hand clothes, old records and electrical equipment, not usually in top working order! It's best to be very careful – a lot of the goods are of doubtful origin.

Mercado municipal 24 de Julho (40)

Cais do Sodré, 1200
☎ 346 29 66
🚋 tram 15, 28
🕐 retail sales

Mon.–Sat. 7am–2pm **wholesale** 5–9.30am **sales to the public** Mon., Wed., Fri. 6–10pm; Tue., Thur. 3–7pm 🏧 🅿 🏧

On Mondays, Wednesdays and Fridays you can buy fresh flowers at this market. Near the Port de Ribeira (not far from the Cais do Sodre) there is a lively fish, fruit and vegetable market

together with other fresh produce from the surrounding districts. Local people often come here to have breakfast after the bars ➡ 64 and night clubs ➡ 72 have closed. ★ The market also has its own restaurant where you can sample some excellent fresh fish. Try the swordfish, grilled sardines or steam-cooked sea bass.

146

do Alecrim to the Rato where you'll find some more antique dealers.

39

43

Solar (41)

70, rua Dom Pedro V, 1250
☎ 346 55 22
➡ 346 55 22
or 342 88 85
🚌 15, 100
🕐 Mon.–Fri.
10am–7pm; Sat.
10am–1pm 🎫

An antique store specializing in old *azulejos* and stones. There is also decorative woodwork (carved angel's heads, flowers), religious figurines and antique Portuguese furniture.

António Trindade (42)

79–81, rua do Alecrim, 1200
☎ 342 46 60
➡ 347 81 93
🚌 15, 100
🕐 Mon.–Fri.
10am–1pm,
2–8pm; Sat.
10am–1pm 🎫

Stylish but often extremely expensive antiques. There are some Portuguese articles, but most are of foreign origin: furniture, porcelain, silver, rugs, light fittings and paintings.

Antiguidades Manuel Murteira (43)

19–21, rua Augusto Rosa, 1100
☎ ➡ 886 38 51
🚌 37, tram 28
🕐 Mon.–Sat. 9am–1pm, 3–7pm 🎫

Another antique shop with a huge variety of quality furniture, paintings, tapestries and sculpture.

➡ Finding your way

Location

Facing the Atlantic Ocean, Lisbon
is the most westerly capital
in Europe (latitude N. 38°43',
longitude W. 9°08').
Lisbon is situated
... 200 miles south of Porto,
... 195 miles northwest of Faro

Useful vocabulary

Avenida : avenue
Beco : cul-de-sac
Cais : quay
Calçada : alley
Escadinhas : steps
Esplanada : esplanade
Estação : station
Jardim : garden
Largo : small square
or alleyway
Parque : park
Praça : square
Rua : road, street
Travessa : crossing

6 Maps

INDEX THE CITY'S DISTRICTS

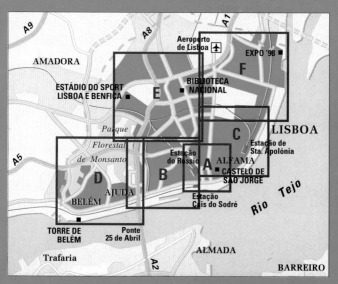

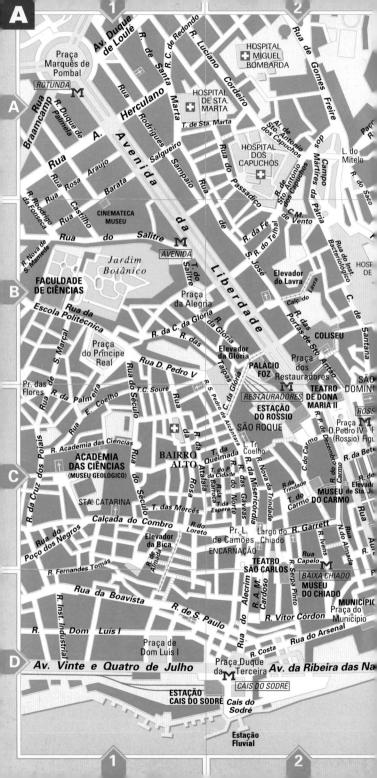

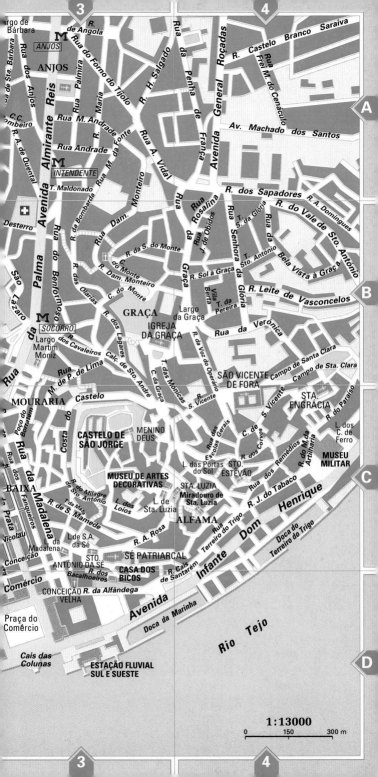

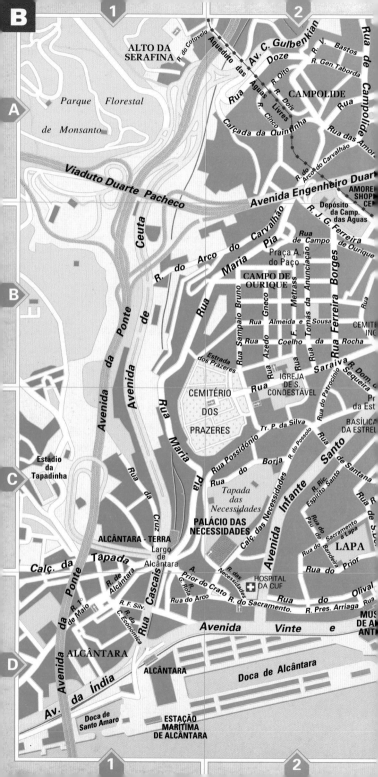

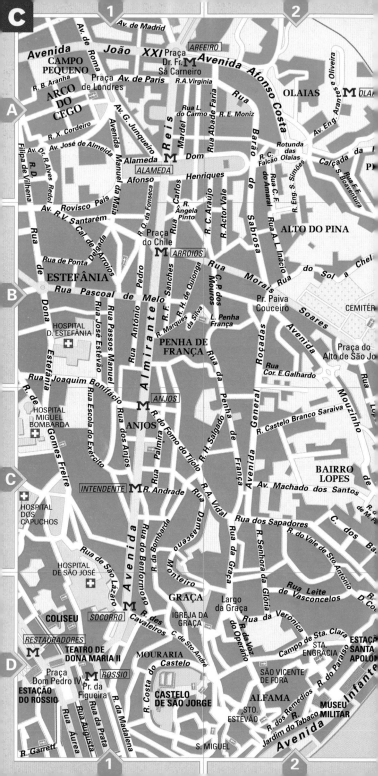

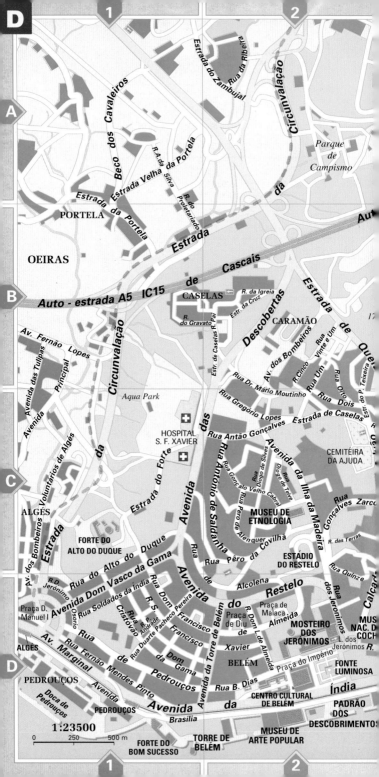

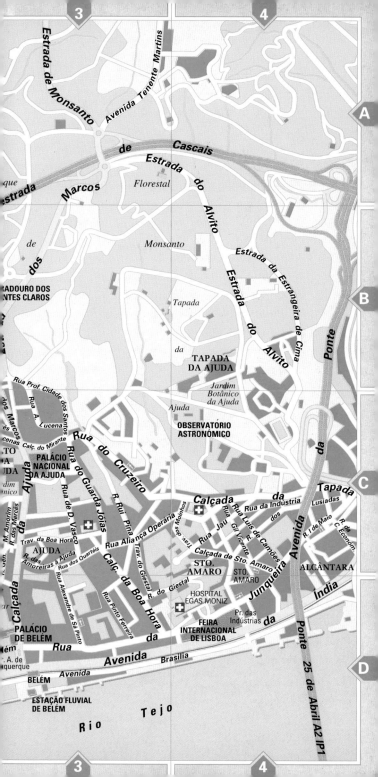

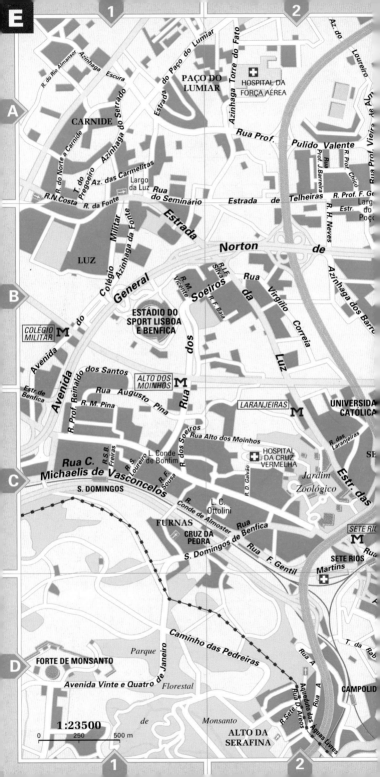

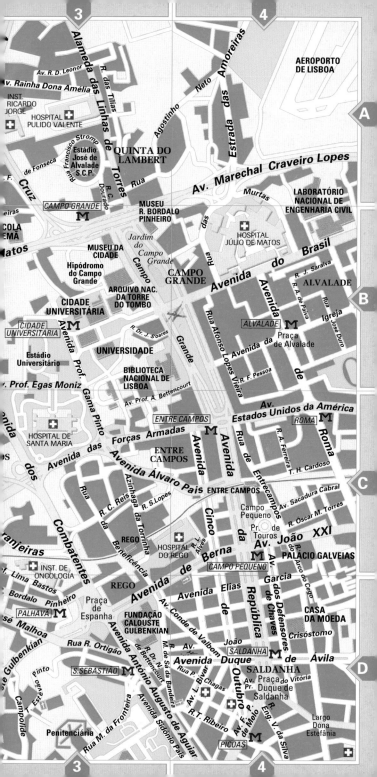

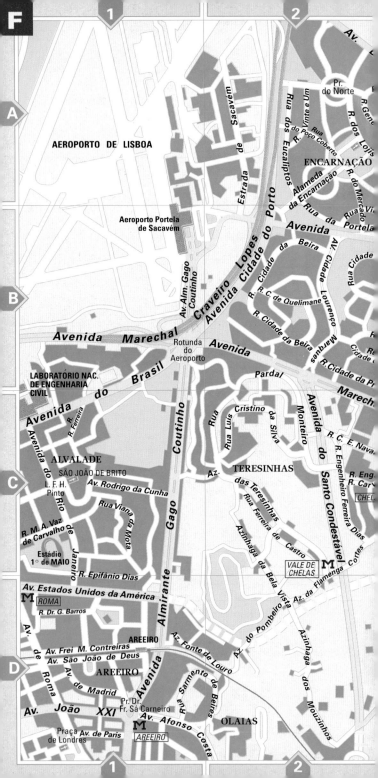

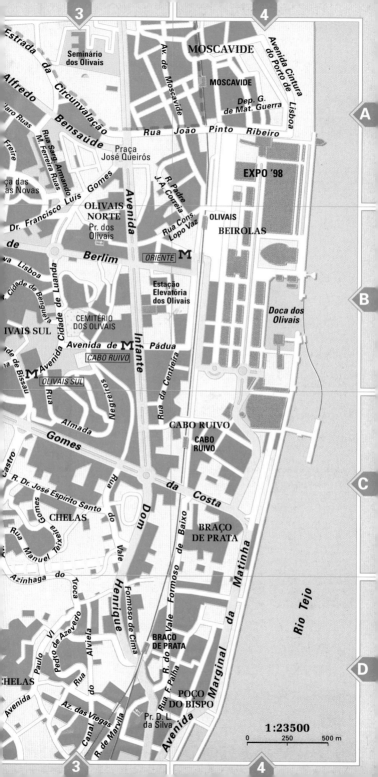

For each street listed below, the information given indicates: the corresponding map (A, B, C, D, E or F) followed by the grid references.

Index
of streets

All the establishments mentioned in this guide along with practical information, tourist attractions and services are listed below.

General
Index

Thanks to Arnaud Février and
Steven Ware for their photographs,
and to all the organizations
mentioned for their invaluable
cooperation.

Picture
Credits